The Occult Roots of Bolshevism

# The Occult Roots of Bolshevism
## From Cosmist Philosophy to Magical Marxism

Stephen E. Flowers

Lodestar
www.seekthemysteries.com

# Contents

Abbreviations —8

Preface: My Four Days as an "Anti-Communist Freedom Fighter" —9

Introduction —15
    Occultism —15
    Magic —16
    Bolshevism —17
    Cosmism —19

1. Roots of Bolshevism —21
    Politics, Philosophy and Religion —22
    Nikolai Fedorov and the Philosophy of the Common Task —24
        Humankind's Common Cause —24
        Transhumanism? —26
    Marxist Philosophy and Theory —29
        The Esoteric Theories of Karl Marx —30
    The Anarchy of Bakunin —38
    The Narodniks —39
    People's Will —40
    Occult Anarchy —40
    Russian Sects and Paganism —41
    Science —44

2. Before Lenin Came: The Russian Silver Age —47
    The Esoteric: From the Satanic to the Cosmic —50
        The Satanic Underground —50
    The Esoteric and the Cosmic —53
    Konstantin Tsiolkovsky —55
    Political Dimensions —57

3. The Age of Lenin —59
    The Occult Lenin —59
    V. D. Bonch-Bruyevich —62
    The Rites and Rituals of Early Bolshevism —63
    Anatoly Lunacharsky and God-Building —70
        God-Building —71
    Alexander Bogdanov —76
        The Proletkult —79
    Gleb Boky and the Search for the Red Shambhala —81
    Mass Murder and the Secret of Social Revolution —83
    Bolshevik Symbolism —84
        The Symbols of Bolshevism —86

4. The Age of Stalin —89
    Stalin and Language —92
    Science in the Age of Stalin —93
    Vladimir Vernadsky —97
    The Continuation of Russian Mysticism —98
    Alexander Chizhevsky —99
    Stalinist Occultism —101
    Stalin's Witch —101
5. Post-Stalinist Ages —103
    Soviet Period after Stalin —103
        Revival of God-Building —103
    The Age of Putin —105
    The Branches and the Root —107
        Alexandr Dugin —107
        Rodnovery —108
    Socialistic Sorcery in the West —111
    Magical Marxism —115
6. General Conclusion and Assessment —117

Appendix: Esoteric Bolshevism and Zoroastrian Tradition —121

Notes —126
Bibliography —127

# Acknowledgements

Special notes of acknowledgement go to Askr Svarte, Cort Williams, Jon Graham, Paul Fredric and Alexandr Dugin.

# Abbreviations

GRU     Main Intelligence Directorate
NBP     National Bolshevik Party
NKVD   The People's Commissariat for Internal Affairs
RSDLP  Russian Social Democratic Labor Party
USSR   Union of Soviet Socialist Republics

# Preface

## My Four Days as an "Anti-Communist Freedom Fighter"

Back when I was in high school in Dallas, Texas I "tried on" many ideologies. I read the *Communist Manifesto*, I became enamored (like Bernie Sanders) with Scandinavian welfare-state politics. But all of this and more were merely youthful explorations of various possibilities. What really grabbed me at the time was the idea of rebellion against Communist dictatorships, and I read about the Hungarian Revolt of 1956 and was inspired by the current events then going on in the Prague Spring in 1968. I fantasized about actually doing things to combat Communist oppression in the Warsaw Pact. Such were the silly youthful fantasies of a sixteen-year-old kid.

After I graduated high school, I traveled to Germany to study the German language at the Goethe Insititut in Prien am Chiemsee. It was there that I became friends with a man who had escaped Hungary in order to study medicine in Germany. He was half German ethnically, and it is a little-known fact today that in that period there was a sort of "affirmative action" program that favored pure Hungarians (or pure Poles, or whatever) in all sorts of avenues of life in the East Bloc countries. German cultural and political domination of the former ethnic enclaves within the Austro-Hungarian Empire was to be "rectified" with such policies. My friend, who now once more lives in his native Hungary as a prosperous physician, had formed a group of buddies, all determined to escape Hungary and go to Germany. All had succeeded but one fellow. (He had a tendency to throw himself going away parties on the eve of his escape, which the police generally found out about.) In any event, my friend wanted to get some vital information to his compatriot about new escape plans. I was asked whether I was willing to go on a *mission* to get this information to him.

On this mission I departed from Vienna, visa in hand, to Budapest. I was to make my way to the town of Szekszárd, several miles south of the capital. I spent a couple of days there meeting with the group. No one seems to have had to work, although, of course it was "illegal" to be unemployed. In retrospect, it was a slackers' paradise. I delivered my messages, return messages were given to me in writing, folded into a small envelope.

One night, there came the proverbial pounding on the door. I was ordered to come to the police station early the next morning. I was questioned, my passport examined and I was ordered to get on the next train out of town and leave Hungary immediately.

The train ride back to Budapest and on to the Austrian border was long and nerve-wracking. I hid and re-hid the envelope several times, before finally sticking it in my underwear. My friend had told me the police would probably not do strip searches or use the rubber hoses on an American. I hoped he was right.

In those days, the trains in Hungary ran on steam. Crossing the border from Hungary into Austria meant stopping for at least an hour, while the engines were switched out. After about fifty-eight minutes, the whistle blew signaling the train was about to depart. I was home free!

But at that moment, the door to the compartment was thrust open and a guard, probably six-foot-six in height appeared and looked at me and said (in German) "Stephen Flowers? Come with me!"

I was taken off the train and escorted by guards with machine guns at the ready to a small building a few feet from the track. How many people had been taken to little buildings like this and never seen again? I wondered as I saw the train speed off toward Austria without me.

I was questioned by one interrogator. Nothing. Everyone left me alone in the room. Time past. I kept still. Someone else came in, same questions new interrogators. All the while, guards with machine guns held high at the door. After more time past, more questions. I was told I could go. I was escorted out to the world's shortest train: an engine and one car. I got in the car. Went to the back of it and sat down. After a minute or two, the door at the front of the car slid open and in stepped a *gnome*— or so he seemed. A very short fellow, all decked out in Alpine gear: *Lederhose*, Tyrolean hat— the whole costume. He sat down at the other end of the car and began to speak in German. He jovially asked me why I had been detained. "I don't know. They thought I had something." He wagered I did have something, and congratulated me on getting away with it. I repeatedly insisted I had nothing, and that it had all been a mistake, a misunderstanding. After a few minutes, he shrugged his shoulders and got up and left through the door he had entered. The doors closed behind him. As I looked out of the window of the train into the now dark, lamp-lit platform outside. I saw the gnome leap from the locomotive and scamper off to that same little building where I had been questioned. The whistle blew. The one-car train departed from the last Hungarian station back to Austria. Finally, I was indeed home free.

I had several other experiences in connection with East Bloc countries over the years, all of which gave me at least some tiny bit of personal experience of a now bygone world, a world which the subject of this book.

So often books which purport to reveal the "occult roots" of a movement or ideology descend into invectives and pejoratives at every turn. My purpose here is not to attack Bolshevism, or to promote it, but rather simply to better understand its roots and branches as viewed from the perspective of decoding its deep-seated cultural and ideological "DNA," if you will. Much of the genius in the way in which Bolshevism initially succeeded lies in the fact that most of its followers were clued in only to how it works, but not necessarily of the underlying factors of why it works. Bolshevism, like National Socialism, historically appears to be better at seizing power than it was at actually running a state in an efficient and effective way. Ultimately, the seizure of power is the prime directive of all such movements. They operate much as warrior-bands, secret orders or cults might have in the past. In reality they primarily exist for the benefit of the high ranking members of the cult exclusively, but most, even in ancient times, were often cunning enough to ascribe their motives and operations to the "greater," or "common," good. Imagine that if you think like what is commonly called a "gangster," what would be the ultimate heist or ultimate scam? Not merely to control and profit from the sale and distribution of contraband goods and services (e.g. illegal drugs, prostitution, gambling) in one or another territory, on some "turf"— but rather to assume control of the *entire* state apparatus and *all* of the means of production in the entire country! This is not to say that movements such as Bolshevism and even National Socialism do no start out with, and are not originally fueled by, what seem to be high ideals — as barbarous or misguided as they might appear today — but that the endowment of such movements with sudden and absolute power tends, as the old saying goes, to corrupt, both suddenly and absolutely.

When an American politician such as Bernie Sanders asserts that America is already a socialist state, (Social Security, Medicare, unemployment benefits, etc.) he has a point, of course, and in a twisted way, the US has also become somewhat of an inverted version of *National* Socialism as well, with ideological features and policies that often give official favor and benefits to certain groups of people based on their immutable *biological* status (regarding race, gender, etc.) Of course, even in this case the main power and benefit always goes to the *leaders* of the political class— not necessarily to the groups their propaganda says they are "fighting for." In this regard, they have cracked the secret code of Bolshevism and learned the practice of Red Magic.

Political movements steeped in the occult and bent on state-craft rarely have as any part of their agenda the teaching or publication of their esoteric doctrines, rather they are only interested in *using* such teachings to gain and hold on to power. For this reason, the esoteric and the occult are usually discouraged or even outlawed in states at the head of which are leaders who have actually employed such occult means to access and maintain that political power.

Throughout the course of this book readers will find themselves regularly seeing parallels between what is being presented and the headlines of today's news regarding politics in the US or other Western "democracies." This is not accidental. The patterns of operation used by the Bolsheviks have seeped into all aspects of culture. The first great influence they had in the West was the inspiration of the movement in Germany called National Socialism.

The world has been "plagued" for years with books about the "occult roots of Nazism." I myself have contributed to this in what I hope is an objective and comprehensive approach in my book *The Occult in National Socialism*. Few have, however, looked into the occult roots of Bolshevism. This is not, as the present book demonstrates, because there are none, but rather it is because such ideas are still concealed for reasons pertaining to domestic Western politics and due to the peculiarities of the history of these roots in the story of Communism in Russia. With the growth of scholarly literature on the subject of Russian Cosmism this picture is gradually changing. The Germans, like the Russians, were well-immersed in occult thinking at the time of these political movements, but Hitler allowed his underlings (Himmler, Darré, Rosenberg, *et al.*) to express themselves independently and thus a huge range of material was left behind. The similarly sometimes tolerant, often intolerant, Lenin only had seven turbulent years in power before control was taken by Stalin— a man who (much to the admiration of Hitler) brooked no dissent to his *steely* will and his slow wit. Some occult dimensions continued, but only in the highest of secrecy. The occult roots of Nazism, like Bolshevism, were promoted and understood only by a minority of the adherents of these movements. For the most part the leaders had to focus entirely on the nuts and bolts of first attaining and then retaining power, making war and meeting the basic needs of the populace, eliminating by various means the troublesome elements of that populace and so had little time or resources for philosophical dreams of those who originally gave rise to such movements themselves. As we will see in the course of this book, leading Bolsheviks in the early phases of the Revolutionary movement were far more deeply involved in Cosmist thinking than Nazi leaders were in any sort of *völkisch* occultism or mysticism. The occult roots of Bolshevism are much clearer and more direct than is the case among National Socialists.

The whole study of Russian occultism, its history and ideology remains somewhat underdeveloped in the West. However, a good deal of impressive work has recently been done. Much of the scarcity of information can clearly be laid at the doorstep of our general lack of knowledge of the Russian language and access to materials. This was the same phenomenon which led to the Russians launching Sputnik to the "surprise" of the West in 1957, despite the fact that they had been publicizing their space program in popular Russian-language magazines for years. Our "intelligence services" just did not pay attention to them and had few trained experts who could read them. I cannot claim to be an expert in the Russian language myself, as many know my areas of expertise lies elsewhere. However, my actual hope for this little book is that it will function as an encouragement for further research by more knowledgeable experts.

Stephen E. Flowers
Woodharrow
May 1, 2021
tilruna72@gmail.com

# Introduction

This book is an exploration of the occult origins of ideas and practices used by the Bolsheviks guided by Vladimir Lenin culminating in the October Revolution of 1917 and the occult branches of that thought process throughout the history of the Soviet Union and beyond to the present moment. For the most part each section of this study is divided into three areas of specific discussion: ideology (politics, philosophy, etc.), science (technology) and occultism proper (psychism, sorcery, etc.). In these divisions, perhaps, I betray my Germanic mode of thought, as Bolshevik philosophy strives for a purely materialistic model and rejects all forms of so-called idealism (a division between "spirit" and "matter").

After this introduction, I will delve into the deep roots of Bolshevism in Marxist theory and Russian culture before the advent of Vladimir Lenin on the stage of Russian history. First the actual Marxist theories upon which Bolshevism is based must be examined, along with other aspects of 19$^{th}$ century ideas of science and occultism, such as Theosophy, which played a surprising role in the esoteric side of many early Revolutionaries and supporters of Lenin. After an interlude on the Russian Silver Age, which was the real cradle of Lenin's philosophy, we will delve directly into the Bolshevik Age with its particular ideas on politics, science and occultism. After Lenin's death, Russia was plunged into two decades of Stalinist repression. But, as we will see, this was not a time period free of occult thinking. Finally, we will visit the world of post-Stalinist occultism in the Soviet and post-Soviet periods.

Before undertaking a study of this kind, it is most important to establish some definitions of certain key words. It is also important that, in the name of reason, we define these words in accordance with the best understanding of the sciences responsible for defining such terms. Perhaps the three most loaded terms used throughout the study are occult(ism), magic and Bolshevism.

## Occultism

For purposes of this study, we will often differentiate between the esoteric and the occult, although for general usages these terms can often be used interchangeably. The esoteric is made up of symbolic traditions about cosmology, anthropology and the history of mankind and the world. Its chief aim is initiation, or the transformation of man both individually and collectively. Occultism, on the other hand is a set of techniques and practices, often connected with esoteric teachings, which enable the practitioner to control the minds of others (e.g. hypnosis), read the future (e.g. clairvoyance, divination, astrology,), to read the destiny or character of another person, to read the past clairvoyantly, to communicate with the dead (e.g. spiritualism), and so on. Following these definitions, the practice of magic acts as a bridge between the esoteric and the occult. **Essential to the definition of the "occult" for purposes of this study is that it is a feature which has been rejected by, or is not (yet) explicable within, the *prevailing* cultural and intellectual norms of a given society.**

## Magic

Another level of the occult is commonly referred to as "magic." In most instances, it might be better called "sorcery." Historically it has not been common for many writers to look at Bolshevism in terms of magic. Ignoring this dimension of the ideology can lead to misunderstanding of how magic works in the modern world. But in order to understand it, the concept of magic must be precisely defined and not be permitted to assume a layman's definition. In current scientific thought, magic is defined as a system of operative meta-communication. Through a form of communication using symbols and symbolic actions various structures of the human psyche can interact with one another, or indeed with the natural or phenomenal world to create effects and changes according to the will and design of the communicator. The Bolsheviks and their ideological heirs initiated this communication loop using speech or linguistics through the *media* of publications, addresses, rallies, broadcasts, the display of certain symbols and signs. All of this is designed to carry a specific and targeted message fashioned to arouse the will of the masses to identify with the directive of the Party program in sufficient numbers to tip the balance of political power in various populations. Clearly the Bolsheviks did attempt to practice a kind of *magic*, but it was in new ways on a more widespread basis than might have been expected.

One can beneficially compare the ways and methods of the Bolsheviks to the National Socialists in Germany. Many of the similarities were in fact due to the manner in which the Nazis "borrowed" from Bolshevik methods. For example, Hitler noted in *Mein Kampf* how the *red* banners of the Communists had a stirring effect on the mind, even if unconsciously, especially when displayed in night-time processions. On this basis, he dictated that the Nazi flag and banners should be predominantly *red* in color.

# Bolshevism

The narrow definition of Bolshevism is that it is the faction of the Russian Social Democratic Labor Party (RSDLP) dominated by V. I. Lenin which was so named by Lenin to imply that his faction was the *majority* of socialists, while the minority was referred to by him as the Mensheviks. The word Bolshevik was little used in an official way after Lenin's faction gained dominance, but the term hung on, especially among detractors of Communism. For my purposes its lack of official meaning or technical definition, other than as a description of Leninism, fits my purpose of having a label that can include all sorts of factions, and have a somewhat romantic and expressly *Russian* ring to it.

The use of language begins with the naming of the parties and factions: Often they use terms such as democratic, socialist, workers, people, liberation and so on in an attempt to give the cause in question a charitable and beneficial aura and take the moral high ground in their struggles. So as mentioned, original and official name of the Bolsheviks was the Russian Social Democratic Labor Party. (Let observers of current American culture take note of the current attempt to insinuate the formula "democratic socialism" into the political debate. Such usages of language in order to "prepare the battlefield" are certainly nothing new.)

The Communist countries almost always display their uses of language in a manipulative way in the very *naming* of the states they control: The Union of Soviet Socialist Republics, The German Democratic Republic, The People's Republic of China, and so on.

Many might object that there was nothing simply "socialistic" about the Soviet government, or that there is nothing "democratic" about East Germany. In fact, the Bolshevik use of language is tantamount to a manipulative art-form— a kind of linguistic sorcery. In the days of the Soviet Union they often spoke of "world peace"— *mir*. (Coincidentally the Russian word *mir* (мир) means both "world" and "peace.") But for them, "peace" meant arriving at a historical point when the entire world would be brought under the governance of one world-wide Soviet system. Then, and only then, would there be "peace." The word *soviet* means "council."

The Communist Party of the Soviet Union grew directly out of Lenin's RSDLP. It would not be until after the Second World War that many of the "Social Democratic" and "Labor" Parties of Europe officially dropped their ideological adherence to Marxism, although they were originally named in such a way that acted as a signal for their actual adherence to Marxist principles.

Lenin's philosophy, which can be called Bolshevism, is outlined in his work *What is to Be Done?* (1901). It delineates the idea that socialist revolution needs to be *organized* and *directed* by a strong professional class of political operatives and that the idea of a completely classless society is impractical in the short term. Here and in the concept that the revolution needs to be led from above and will not simply occur on its own as a matter of historical dialectical evolution his ideas run counter to Marxist theory. But this Leninist innovation was essential to Revolutionary success for socialist parties everywhere and allowed for the movement to become an engine for the overthrow of countries (usually by violence) and the confiscation of the entire means of production and the governmental institutions of various states under the direct control and management of the intelligentsia of the Party. This created an administrative structure that would inspire virtual political war-lords from Mao to Castro as well as their pale and plodding admirers in Western republics. The insistence on the scientific *correctness* of the historical dialectic and the idea that the cause was a *just* one in liberating the oppressed workers, peasants, etc., from their bondage was designed to provide such movements with the "high ground" both intellectually and morally.

It was a common misconception, even back in the days of the USSR and the Warsaw Pact, that all the people in these countries must belong to the "communist party." Actually, to belong to the Communist Party in these countries and republics was an honor and a privilege which had to be sought and earned, or one had to be invited to join. Typically, membership only amounted to about ten percent of the population. This too is where a degree of occultism comes in. The Party was very much akin to a fraternity, a fraternal order of the ruling elite. In the USSR, the streets of Moscow were almost devoid of automobiles. If you saw one, it was probably being driven by or for a Party member. The most conspicuous scene was that of a motorcade of ZIL-114s heading across the city from the country-side toward the Kremlin. Communist "royalty" was coming to town. The "trick" of living and thriving in these countries was to become part of this elite, and within that there was yet another elite— those who could both think and survive. Half of the Party members were perfunctory and obedient apparatchiks (operatives) who had proven their unthinking loyalty to the party and its "group-think" from an early age— useful, but expendable. The "magicians" were the thinkers in the Party. There were many of these in the Lenin era, few at the time of Stalin.

# Cosmism

The decentralized ideology of Cosmism(1) developed secretly during the years when Marxism itself was being developed. It did not come into general view until around the time of the first revolution of 1905. Actually, Russian Cosmism is a designation that has only relatively recently (after the mid-1960s) been applied to a wide range of ideas produced by Russian thinkers beginning in the 19th century. There is no orthodox definition. How could there be, so many of the earlier writers were dedicated Symbolists and Anarchists!

When it comes to discussing the various individuals who have been exponents of the Cosmist way of thinking in one way or another there is a certain problem about when to place them in the narrative of history. It will be found that some did not publish in their life-times (Fedorov) but were influential in life as well as later, others entered upon the stage of history and perished roughly in the same period (e.g. Bogdanov) while others were active but kept a low profile or were able to avoid the landmines of political orthodoxies established during the Stalinist era and survived to tell the tale.

There was always something that might be called the Russian Philosophy that was in one way or another touched by the mind of Nikolai Fedorov. This came to be called "Cosmism." This term was only used later — especially after the 1980s — to attempt to group together what was really a diverse group of thinkers, writers, poets, artists, religious mystics, atheistic revolutionaries, politicians and most especially scientists, and to discover their common bonds as Russian Cosmists. The definition of Cosmism is dependent on the understanding of a set of what the writer Michael Hagemeister calls "genetic marks." These are discussed by George M. Young (2012: 7-11). I will summarize them here.

Cosmism must be understood as an approach to *active evolution*. It is holistic, anthropocentric and at the same time cosmocentric. Its aim or direction is one of an all-inclusive perfected wholeness within the context of what came to be called the noosphere. The noosphere is the "space" which contains, or acts as a matrix for, beings with reasoning capacity. Eduard Suess coined the term "biosphere" in 1885, but it was more popularized by the Russian Vladimir Ivanovich Vernadsky and indicated the space in which living beings exist, and Vernadsky further refined the concept by positing the noosphere— a stage in evolution beyond the limitations of the biosphere. Cosmism aims for the overcoming of all disease processes, and death itself leading to the development of an immortal and perfected human race. Cosmism also is pointedly not limited to the confines of the planet Earth, but rather enthusiastically promotes the idea of inter-planetary colonization. In a paradoxical manner, the movement known as Cosmism is also seen as a peculiarly *Russian* one and so bears the marks of a certain degree of ethnocentrism.

Resources concerning Russian Cosmism are increasingly appearing in English. See the bibliography of this book for some of these. The online journal *e-flux* frequently contains articles of interest on this topic.

Some readers may find the connections between Bolshevism and Cosmism to be disingenuous. To those I have two things to say: First of all, the number of Cosmist ideas that were held by early Bolsheviks and the fact that Cosmists of various stripes were important in the Bolshevik ranks throughout the history of the Soviet Union speaks to the actuality of the connection. Secondly, as in a certain sense this book is a continuation of an intellectual discussion about the "occult roots" of various other movements, such as National Socialism in Germany, the role of occult thinking is just as much, if not more so, a feature of Russian Bolshevist thinking than it ever was of Nazism.(2)

When we come to examine the occult roots of Bolshevism we must do so with a wide-angle lens that takes into account a precise understanding of what terms such as occultism and magic actually mean as well as have a deep understanding of the true nature of what Bolshevism was and is. We also need to come to some understanding of the idea of Russian Cosmism. All this is the aim and topic of this book. Some will find it inspiring, others incendiary. The text is not intended as an attack on, or support for, Bolshevism as such, but only as a tool for understanding this major phenomenon, thought by many to have been relegated to ash-heap of history in the early 1990s, but whose spirit still lives and motivates many to action even today.

# 1. Roots of Bolshevism

The Bolsheviks of the October Revolution of 1917 had evolved out of a long history of developments in the 19<sup>th</sup> century. Bolshevism began as a particularly Russian form of ideology, with deep roots in German philosophy as well as Russian experience and history. To understand the complexity of the culture which gave direct rise to Bolshevism, we need to understand the soils out of which it grew.

The early 19<sup>th</sup> century was a time when the Industrial Revolution (ca. 1760-1840) had reached an advanced level of development in some regions. People moved from the farms to the urban areas where factories, and hence work, was available. For centuries peasants and serfs had been exploited in the countryside, now these people were moving into cities, where those patterns were repeating themselves. People, not just men but also women and often children, worked in harsh conditions for little money. There was some upward mobility for educated individuals, and a new so-called middle class was slowly developing. But for the most part it was the *working class* that was most rapidly increasing in numbers. The exploitation of humans and the environment, the careless despoiling of the land was something that had been predicted by the Romantics, such as Mary Shelley in her books *Frankenstein* and *The Last Man*.

The secret of the history of esoteric Bolshevism is that its roots are complex but hidden under a veneer of Marxist ideological orthodoxy. In fact, there are three roots upon which it stands: Russian nativism (pagan, Orthodox and sectarian), Cosmism (religious and secular) and Marxism (both Leninist and Trotskyite). The importance and persistence of this system of roots is dramatically revealed after the fall of the Soviet Union— when native Slavic religion (Rodnovery) and Cosmism began to surge upward in the consciousness of the Russian people after having been deprived of nutrients for seventy-five years.

The grandfather of Russian Cosmism was Nikolai Fedorov (also transliterated Fyodorov) (1828-1903). He and his ideas will be seen to lurk beneath the surface of Russian intellectual culture both during his own lifetime as well in the years that followed his death. Running virtually parallel to the life of Fedorov was that of the German philosopher Karl Marx (1818-1883), together with his collaborator Friedrich Engels (1820-

1895). Marxist philosophy made its way into largely agrarian Russia only slowly. In the mid- to late-19th century the Russian intelligentsia was enamored with the Narodnik Movement, Nihilism, the Anarchy of Mikael Bakunin (1814-1876) and a truly Marxist-based socialist movement was only instituted with the founding of the Soviet Union in 1917. So, throughout the 19th century the two streams of thought which would manifest as both Russian Cosmism and Marxist-Leninism were developing just below the surface.

The ideas of both the Cosmists, proto-Cosmists and the Socialists were all developed during the course of the 19th century in a time of great intellectual upheaval in which old ideas based on religious dogmas and political conventions were being overturned in the name of science and supposedly rational thought. As in every case in which "new" ideas are introduced into a culture, the old ideas have to be called into question, and even discredited or overthrown. This usually happens naturally as events and advances in thought occur, but the Marxists will eventually develop a Revolutionary science in which such processes are brought increasingly under the control and guidance of a centralized ideological authority.

Focus needs to be placed on the situation in Russia during the 19th century and the unique position of Russia in history at that time understood. Orthodox Marxist theory held that socialism would only take root and become successful once an industrialized capitalistic system failed. As Russia had not yet been heavily industrialized, it was thought by orthodox Marxists of the West to be a poor candidate for revolution. The ideas of Fedorov and Marx in many ways were certainly miles apart. But in certain key factors they touched upon one another. Their stated goals were similar, their methods different and their underlying culture and temperament profoundly at odds.

## Politics, Philosophy and Religion

Russia in the 19th century was a world in which the intelligentsia was closely connected to all the various cultural developments in Europe, but whose enormous lower echelons of society (the peasants ["serfs"], workers and common poor) were hopelessly disconnected from the intellectual, cultural and economic resources that were being enjoyed by the average middle class person in France, Germany or England. The tension between this intelligentsia and the under-classes was a slow burning fuse that would reach its inevitable conclusion in the events of 1917.

After the final defeat of Napoleon and thus the end of the Napoleonic Wars under the leadership of Tsar Alexander I in 1815 Russia was beset with a new array of challenges politically and culturally as the tsar's younger brother Nicholas I came to power. The rest of the century was an ongoing struggle between the forces demanding reform and modernization, liberation of the serfs and some sort of democratic institutions and those Imperial forces bent upon maintaining the *status quo* — as much as possible.

Russia was historically very open to ideas flowing in from both Germany and France. Specifically, the most powerful philosophical influences were from Germany with the writings of Hegel, Schelling and then Marx and Engels. Various Russian thinkers and writers actively influenced the intellectual development of the country in the 19th century. These stemmed from a wide variety of schools: Existentialism, Symbolism, Anarchism and Socialism. Alexander Herze is said to be the "father of Russian socialism," and Georgi Plekhanov the first true Marxist there. Of course, Russian Cosmism was developing and Slavophilic movements were strong, including that known as Pechvennichestvo ("return to the native soil") which was influenced by the Russian Orthodox Church. It should also be noted that three of the most important and influential occultists of the time, Helena Blavatsky, George Gurdjieff and Peter Ouspensky had their roots in the Russian Empire.

Russia was religiously dominated by the Russian Orthodox Church with its seat in Moscow — envisioned as the "New Rome" to be the center of a great empire. As is usually the case when a culture is so dominated by one set of dogmas, sects and heretical off-shoots abounded in secret and hidden corners. It is often found that even among the most radical sorts of reformers and social rebels — such as Leo Tolstoy and Nikolai Fedorov an adherence to the Russian Orthodox faith was often passionate. It appears that this faith even had its adherents within the officially atheistic leadership of the Communist Party right up to the end. During the funeral of the next to last general Secretary of the Communist Part of the USSR, Konstantin Chernenko in 1985, his widow, Anna Dmitriyevna could be seen bending over the body and openly performing Russian Orthodox prayers.

George M. Young (2012: 27-45) provides a succinct and insightful summary of the esoteric world of Russia in the years leading up to the Revolution and in the context of the ideas of Nikolai Fedorov. One cannot fail to be impressed with the complexity and level of intensity this culture expresses in regard to things esoteric, magical and philosophical.

# Nikolai Fedorov
## and the Philosophy of the Common Task

Nikolai Fedorov (1829 –1903) was the offspring of a noble house who studied at the Richelieu Lyceum in Odessa and became a teacher in several small Russian towns before taking up a position at the Rumyantsey Museum as a librarian in 1878. He quietly worked there for the rest of his life. He wrote, thought and discussed ideas with others, but published nothing during his life-time. His ideas, seen as foundational to the Russian Cosmist Movement, only gained widespread attention with the posthumous appearance of selected writings between 1906 and 1913 edited by his students and entitled *Philosophy of the Common Task* (also known as *Philosophy of Physical Resurrection*).

We are extremely lucky to have studies such as that of George Young (2012) and the anthology of material edited by Boris Groys (2018) to guide us through the byways of Russian Cosmism.

Despite the fact that Fedorov thought of himself as a devout Christian, he was also a dedicated *futurist* whose theories were aimed toward the eventual perfection of humanity and its society. These ideas included immortality and even the revival and immortalization of the dead. For someone who did not even publish anything in his own life-time Fedorov's influence was nevertheless profound. He is rightly considered the father and chief original thinker of Russian Cosmism.

## Humankind's Common Cause

Fedorov saw that evolution itself was a teleological process directed toward an expansion of intelligence or consciousness. Mankind was seen as not only the apex of evolution, but at this point also an active participant in its management. For Fedorov, human mortality was at once the greatest sign of man's imperfection and the very *cause* of the evil acts and motivations which plague the history of mankind. In this Fedorov follows along with the reasoning of Biblical thought: Adam sinned (with disobedience) and was punished by death, by mortality. Fedorov saw the task of all of humankind as immortalization— as a cause it will unite all peoples regardless of race or class.

Fedorov thought that human beings died for two reasons: one internal and one external to the entity itself. Internally, the body is incapable of infinitely renewing itself. To conquer this circumstance a method of psychophysiological regulation needs to be developed. The external reason has to do with the destructive character of the surrounding environment. In order to overcome this, the environment — Nature itself — has to be regulated. This will be done by infusing will and reason into Nature. This will involve the prevention of natural disasters, control of the environment, destruction of viruses, perfection of solar power and the exploration of space where humans will have the opportunity to express their creativity on a cosmic scale. These Cosmist ideas all sound very familiar today.

For Fedorov the Common Task of Immortality had two inseparable sides: First there was the attainment of physical immortality for all people living at present, the second part was the actual resurrection of all of those who had lived in the past. His scientific imagination was greatly tempered with a sense of ethics and justice for all. Fedorov saw the necessity for the resurrection and immortalization of the dead as a moral or ethical imperative. It would simply be unjust for the currently living to attain immortality while leaving their ancestors who had given them life to remain dead! For Fedorov complete victory only comes when all have been transformed in order to attain immortality and perfection.

Fedorov's efforts were aimed at planning future scientific research toward the restoration of life to the dead and causing this revivification to become a permanent state. Clearly, Fedorov had it in mind that human ingenuity and science would be the mode by which the "resurrection of the dead" promised by religion would be made a reality. In many ways, Fedorov prefigured the idea of what we call "cloning" today. He also described a form of immortalization along genetic-hereditary lines. Here revival could be achieved in successive re-births along genetic lines— the son would revive the father. In this it seems that he was re-discovering the ancient Indo-European mode of "reincarnation" whereby the descendants are seen to be ancestors reborn. The "genetic twin" of the dead person would then have to have the old memories and mentalities re-installed. Here we are also reminded of the rituals and methods used by Tibetan Buddhists to discover the new incarnation of the recently deceased Dalai Lama and how they then undertake exercises to reawaken awareness of identity of the dead Dali Lama in his supposed newly reincarnated self. Interestingly, all this did not merely involve a reproduction of the body of the dead person, as it was a flawed and imperfect form to begin with, but rather it had to do with the Remanifestation of the mind of the individual in a new and more perfect physical vehicle capable of infinite renewal. Those who are still living would undergo a parallel process of perfection and immortalization. It is uncanny the degree to which these ideas mirror those suggested by Zoroastrian teachings of the resurrection of the dead. (This is the source from which the Judeo-Christian tradition borrowed the idea.)

All of these apparently fantastic developments were to be achieved, according to Fedorov by means of general scientific studies of aging, death and postmortem studies liberated from all restrictions and not by any miraculous divine intervention.

It is remarkable the degree to which Russian Cosmism accords with the Zoroastrian ideology which holds that humans are co-creators with the deity and that development of the rational mind and the practical applications of these developments will lead to human perfection and happiness. For more on this see the Appendix in this book. What makes it all the more remarkable is that the Russian people, and Slavs in general, developed in close cooperation with Northern Iranian peoples, such as the Scythians, Sarmatians and Alans.

## Transhumanism?

Another recent idea for which Fedorov was certainly preparer of the way is that which is currently called "Transhumanism." Many aspects of what has been attached to the concept of Transhumanism are actually foreign to Fedorov's ideas, however. He did recognize that humans have always needed to account for the deficits in the human physical form. This has always been done with "technology." This is true whether we talk about weapons accounting for our weak teeth or finger nails, or automobiles for our weak and slow legs, or eventually airplanes because we cannot fly. More advanced technologies will continue this trend and we will develop a "prosthetic" civilization. This will make what had been done with external tools part of our organic beings. He envisioned a future where humans will develop new organs and even cease to have to feed themselves as they become entirely autotrophic, self-feeding creatures. He even envisioned the possibility of humans acquiring energy from the environment in a perpetual loop of exchange. In all of this, however, Fedorov always saw the supremacy of the mind, or "spirit," if you will, as the source for all of these developments

As mentioned, it was only after Fedorov's death in 1903 that his students began to gather and publish his works under the title *Philosophy of the*

*Common Task.* These publications continued until the coming of Soviet times.

Fedorov's ideology of the Common Task is outlined in bold strokes by Michael Hagemeister (1997, p. 189):

> Nowhere is the goal of overcoming death and resurrecting the dead given more detailed treatment than in Fedorov's description of the "common task," and nowhere is this goal based on firmer moral conviction. As a rational being, man is able, indeed obliged, to work to transform everything natural (and therefore transitory) including himself and his external environment into his control and turning it into a work of art, man rids himself of all divisiveness, destruction and mortality. Upon humans' actions depends not only their own deliverance but also the salvation and perfection of the entire universe.
>
> The realization of Fedorov's project does not, however, presume to restrict itself to "superhuman" individuals or to a select group of chosen ("the righteous"). On the contrary: the combined efforts of all humankind, living and dead, are required in order to vanquish death and perfect the universe, since perfection and immortality are morally justified only if all without exception are comprehended in the action intended to nullify historically accumulated injustice and suffering. Thus all "brothers" are called upon to unite fraternally and combine all of their scientific and technical skills in the project of physically resurrecting their deceased forefathers. Fedorov's innerworldly paradise attains perfection through the unification of all humankind— a paradise created by and for all, in which there are no damned, no victims of history.
> The means of attaining "all-unity" lies in the resurrection that mankind consciously effects with the help of science and technology and that is progressively directed toward the conscious re-creation (*soznatel'noe vossozdanie*) of all our ancestors. Fedorov regards this as an exclusively physical process— tracking down, collecting, and synthesizing the smallest of particles. The product is a consummate work of art that, as the creation of a rational being, is immortal and perfect.

In so many ways Cosmism appears to be a system in which certain extremely ancient Zoroastrian ideas meet the Space Age— but it is in a very conscious way a totally *Russian* way of thinking.

> Originally, Cosmism developed roughly around the same time as Marxism through the musings of Nikolai Fedorov, born in 1829, a philosopher and librarian who worked at the Rumyantsev Library in Moscow, the first public museum and library in Russia. It affected visual

artists, poets, filmmakers, theatre directors, novelists (Tolstoy and Dostoevsky read and were friends with Fedorov), architects, composers, Soviet politics, value systems, and many forms of speculative futurist technology. It offered itself as an alternative worldview, an odd visionary attempt to solve problems relating to humankind's condition on earth. By the nineteen thirties Stalin forbade it, as a number of its practitioners had regrettably aligned with Leon Trotsky, and he jailed, exiled, or murdered its most prominent adherents. But Cosmism was not totally eradicated, and has returned to permeate swaths of what is referred to in Russian as the "intelligentsia."

Ellen Pearlman 2019 p. 85

It would be a mistake to limit Bolshevism to Marxism. Bolshevism is a particularly Russian synthesis of Marxist ideology. It is, of course, also known as Marxism-Leninism. But when we look for the occult roots of such ideologies we have to look at the forces that shaped these two thinkers as well as study the active participants in these two ideologue's intellectual lives. Marx was a product of German academia and the Hegelian School, while Lenin was the living manifestation of Russian Bohemian culture stemming from the Tsarist Empire's Silver Age. Many of the deep roots of Bolshevism reach back into the soil of Germany and in the academic world of that mecca of philosophy and science in the 19$^{th}$ century.

Fedorov had several important friendships or associations with other thinkers, writers and scientists who to some extent or another were influenced by him. One of the most important of these was the great Russian writer Leo Tolstoy (1828-1910). They were quite close in the 1880s and early 1890s. However, Fedorov cut off the relationship in 1892 over "political" differences. Tolstoy openly criticized the Russian government and church, while Fedorov remained a true conservative with undivided loyalties to the institutions of state.

Fedorov influenced many others in his private teachings. These ideas are said to have been influential on Peter Ouspensky, who was at one point linked with Gurdjieff. He was also personally linked with Fyodor Dostoyevsky. One of Fedorov's students was also the rocket scientist named Konstantin Tsiolkovsky, about whom I will say more later. Tsiolkovsky was a scientific visionary as regards space travel and by about 1903 he had conceived of rockets, space suits and the plan for people from earth colonizing the planets of the solar system. To summarize, Fedorov was a futurist of the most radical sort but he also a devout adherent of the Russian Orthodox Church. He fostered such ideas as the perfection of the human race and society, that humans could be made immortal physically and that the dead could actually be physically resurrected— all through *scientific* means applied by human reason. He also posited the necessity of the colonization of space as well as of the underwater regions of the earth.

## Marxist Philosophy and Theory

While Fedorov's ideas were being spread privately and in secret throughout much of the 19<sup>th</sup> century, the ideology of Marx and Engels was being published in widely disseminated and vigorously promoted forms.

Bolshevism would become a specific branch of Marxism. But one cannot understand Bolshevism without first understanding the underlying philosophy of Karl Marx. In turn the essence Marxism is to be seen as a further development of the philosophy of Georg W. F. Hegel. Hegel is best known from his development of the idea of the dialectic: thesis-antithesis and synthesis. Hegel was, however, also an *idealist*. The so-called Young Hegelians who were in one way or another students of Hegel combined the dialectic with purely positivistic materialism, rejecting all forms of "idealism" which might imply that there was more to the world than could be seen, weighed and measured. Marxism has deep philosophical roots that seem to go back all the way to the Greek Epicureans, about whom Marx wrote his doctoral dissertation.

Already at the conclusion of the 18<sup>th</sup> century the whole medieval order of European thought was being called into serious question by certain thinkers, especially in France. These included men such as Jean-Jacques Rousseau, the Marquis de Sade and Julien Offray de la Mettrie. These were all serious spiritual or intellectual rebels or dissenters. The Devil or Satan seen as the archetypal rebel against the prevailing order of the world made him a perennial symbol of revolution in the 19<sup>th</sup> century. This was true even among the materialist/positivist revolutionaries who also saw Satan as a hero.

The ancient philosophy of Epicureanism was revived in the mid-nineteenth century fueled by a new form of materialism theoretically pioneered by Julien Offray de la Mettrie. German critics and philologists had already cast great doubt on the truth of the Bible. God was called into question on all fronts. This new materialism would be melded with the philosophy of Georg Hegel and the whole system would then be projected into the world of economic and political action. The assertion that the material universe is all that exists, and any notion of a metaphysical realm is purely an aberration or delusion, is in and of itself, a matter of faith in something unseen or unapparent. In practice radical materialism is just as "mystical" as spiritualism, and history has shown that it is no more "scientific" than theology and often not nearly as effective. Things which are scientific, are verifiable and repeatable. They are the results of the application of a scientific principle which results in reliable and predictable outcomes. Such has never been the case historically as regards the application of Marxist principles.

The materialists of the 19th century were all rebellious revolutionaries — intellectual as well as political. Everywhere in Europe there ruled a King, Kaiser or Czar, and their own political rationale for their place in the political world was that they were placed in their positions by God. Since their political positions were couched in Biblical metaphors in cultures which had for centuries been dominated by Christian imagery, it is therefore not surprising that when their positions were called into question that their critics might even tend to show an overwhelming amount of sympathy for the Devil.

## The Esoteric Theories of Karl Marx

Karl Marx did not invent socialism, communism or historical materialism, but he was an original synthesizer and codifier of a range of philosophical, economic and socio-political ideas into a theoretically coherent whole. This ideology was then able to be utilized and more forcefully disseminated than had ever been the case with the informal association of concepts that marked related pre-Marxist movements.

Careful historical analysis shows that the deep occult roots of Marxism actually lie in Hermetic philosophy. Erica Lagalisse (2019) points to the work of Glenn Magee (2002) as tracing the Hermetic origins of Hegel's thought, and out of Hegel's theories concerning the dialectic Marx developed the underlying principles of his historical or material dialectic. In the history of ideas Marx can be said to have materialized or secularized the philosophy of Hegel, which was originally much closer to the idealism of Plato. This is a reflection of the general trend in philosophy toward materialism or "positivism" throughout the course of the 19th century.

Marx was born in Trier, Germany on 5 May 1818 to an ethnically Jewish family. (Berlin 1963 pp. 21-22.) His father, Heinrich, had converted to Lutheranism in the year just before Karl's birth. The boy was brought up entirely within the Lutheran faith and was diligent in his religious studies.

In 1835, he began to study law in Bonn, but transferred to Berlin the following year. There he was quickly "converted" to the study of philosophy under the influence of the "Young Hegelians." This was the group of intellectuals engaged in the task of transforming of the principles of Hegel's historical *idealism* into historical *materialism*.

It was his original plan to become a university professor. Marx wrote his doctoral dissertation on the philosophy of the Epicureans, who were early proponents of a materialistic cosmology. Prussian political surveillance and policing of the academic world in Berlin and the various German states in the east forced Marx to go west to Saarbrücken, where he met a man named Moses Hess who was a socialistic Jewish nationalist (precursor to Zionism). Hess is said to have had significant influence on both Marx and Engels, but he was left behind as the other two developed their philosophy of Communism. Marx soon became the editor of a liberal newspaper, the *Rheinische Zeitung*, where Moses Hess worked and the paper was significantly radicalized. The paper was suppressed by the government and Marx had to flee to Paris, but he was also expelled from France in 1845, eventually settling in England. In 1848, Marx wrote one of his two major works -- in collaboration with Engels — *The Manifesto of the Communist Party*. He lived the rest of his life in relative obscurity in London.

In 1864, the first congress of the International Workingman's Association was held in London. This was a federation of various unions and radical organizations. Marx was able to exert a tremendous amount of influence on this group. He imposed his vision of an international and disciplined federation of radical organizations with the intention to destroy capitalist society. Because he held generally authoritarian principles, Marx was opposed to the plan proposed by the Russian anarchist Mikail Bakunin, who was at the time almost as prestigious a thinker as Marx.

Marx began to publish his second great work, and *magnum opus*, entitled *Capital: A Critique of Political Economy* (*Das Kapital: Kritik der politischen Ökonomie*) in 1867. This was only the first of what would reach four volumes, with the last three volumes being published after his death from extensive notes edited by his intellectual partner, Friedrich Engels. This ponderous work was replete with complex mathematical formulas proving his theories of historical materialism, economics and the historical dialectic as being *correct* in a virtually "mathematical" sense.

Toward the end of his life, Marx developed some closer ties with Russian Communists. But before these ties could be exploited, he died in London on 14 March 1883. He is buried in Highgate Cemetery. For the most part, his work remained theoretical and largely impractical, but within it was encoded a formula for gaining political power. It would take the ruthless cunning of Lenin to put the theories into practical use in the Revolutionary movement in Russia, culminating in the overthrow of the Tsar and the establishment of the Union of Soviet Socialist Republics following the 1917 Revolution.

As is well-known, Marx's attitude toward traditional religion was that it should be considered "the opiate of the masses." Ultimately it would be the ideal for the philosophy espoused by Marx to replace entirely that part of human life formerly reserved for "religion." This antipathy toward religion was really just a sort of *avant-garde* way of thinking popular in universities among the elite of academia in the early nineteenth century. He fell in with a group at the University of Berlin called the *Doktorklub*, who were all "Young Hegelians." Their aim was an atheistic program intended to destroy the superstructure of conservative authority. Religion was a major part of this. Later he concentrated on economic theories coupled with historical materialism, but Marx originally had a vision of the "total redemption of humanity," (Riemer 1987, p. 64) as he indicated in the introduction to his *Contribution to the Critique of Hegel's Philosophy of Right* (1844). The effect of Marxist philosophy can be called "prophetic politics" in which a total *transformation* of the state and world is envisioned— and then enacted.

Early themes of Marxian thought, where the foundations of his motivations might be discovered, have been called Faustian and/or Promethean in nature. (Kolakowski 1981, pp. 409; 412; 414.) Even the casual observer will have noticed the quasi-religious features of Marxism both as a theory and as it has been practiced in various countries in the 20th century. All this is best revealed in his own very early writings, e.g. his epic drama *Oulanem* (1837) and his poetry. In one of these poems, "The Fiddler" ["*Der Spielmann*"] (1841), he writes:

> Behold, my blood-blackened saber shall stab
> Without fail into your heart.
>> God neither knows nor does he honor art.
> It rises into the brain as vapors from Hell.
> Until my brain is deluded and my heart transformed:
> I bought it while still alive from the Dark-One.
>> He beats the time for me, he gives the signs;
>> must more boldly, madly rush in the March of Death...

(ll. 17-24)

Marxism outlines a system which can be described as mystical materialism. He posits that history is driven by an organic or mechanical substructure and that its evolution is impelled not by the mind of *God*, as Hegel would have had it, but by exclusively *material* considerations, e.g. purely economic determination or human behavior and the change caused by struggles between economically determined *classes* in society. Culturally we are now so deeply submerged in Marxist thinking ourselves that the *mystical* component of this idea has disappeared from our conscious awareness. What, if not "God," is responsible for this unseen set of immutable and inexorable laws? Throughout all of history, classes of people — as determined by economic status — who were without power would, by the inevitable *force* of this mysterious historical dialectic, wrest power away from those who have it at present. Better said, this power would inevitably devolve to them, but they could, if they awaken to the laws which Marx reveals, hasten the process through Revolution. In the end the proletariat would, by the sheer force of the historical dialectic, overcome the over-ripe, and on-the-verge-of-rotting, capitalist establishment.

Supposedly, history as determined by economic class, would proceed through stages of development determined mechanistically by the historical dialectic. The first level is that of slave-societies (such as ancient Greece and Rome), these were inevitably overcome by the feudalistic order and a new phase of history was introduced. The feudal order was brought down by the capitalists in conjunction with the Industrial Revolution. The powerful capitalists exploit the relatively powerless proletariat, but inevitably the proletariat will evolve their power and overcome the capitalists. These forces of the historical dialectic work mechanically and materialistically according to certain virtually mathematical or algebraic formulas. The purpose and role of socialist revolution is merely to aide history in its development. The Revolution then installs a *Socialist* state which through (re-)education, force, and if need be, genocide, will create the circumstances for the arrival of a truly *Communist* state— one in which (theoretically) no laws would be necessary property would be held in common and world peace would reign.

Marx always claimed that his theories were purely "scientific" or rationally based, that he merely had the clearest view of historical change and its causes. His masterpiece, *Das Kapital* has pages of algebraic-type equations in which he claims to outline the mathematical certainty and *correctness* of his economic and historical theories. These mathematical equations, and the numeric certainty which they imply, are the origin of the very idea of "political correctness" which has entered into popular jargon today. Marx tried to claim that he was *correct*, not so much in a moral sense, but in a mathematical one. In fact, his elaborate equations functioned not so much as mathematics as they did as magical sigils meant to bedazzle the mind of the reader or observer to be convinced that Marx must indeed be correct.

In its simplest form the Marxist equation to determine political correctness, which later was applied outside questions of economics and economic class-conflicts to embrace any and all social, racial, political, cultural and even *biological* issues is:

$$\text{Time}$$
$$- \text{Power} \quad \rightarrow \quad + \text{Power}$$

Any entity, being, organization, etc. relatively lacking in power (here designated as *minus* power) is *destined* by the historical dialectic to inherit power over time. "The meek shall inherit the earth." Looked at on a physical level, this equation runs counter to nature. Usually things move from high pressure to low pressure, power is a positive charge that moves into a vacuum where power is lacking. This sort of *lex talonis* was actually used by Lenin in practical tactical situations, but by using Marxist theory he was able to take a theoretical "moral high ground" assumed as a strategic move. The root of how this could be broadly interpreted as a moral high ground is found in the attitude apparently found in the Beatitudes ("Sermon on the Mount). Curiously, this text seems to have been generally misinterpreted by Greek translators who did not quite understand the Aramaic of the original, and who made a whole "new sense" out of the text.

The problem with using terms such as "mathematical," "correct," or "scientific" in connection with these concepts is that there is *nothing scientific about them.* They are symbolic, philosophical and subjective creations which make their actual appeals in a poetic, mythic and even magical way based on how *persuasive* and appealing they are. They are entirely mystical, not scientific. This does not mean they are not effective.

As Marx theoretically posited it, the changes he predicted were a matter of historical inevitability. The Revolutionary is there merely to help history along in its march to Socialism and eventually to Communism. It can always be argued that to be on the side of the relatively powerless ( −power) entity in any struggle or conflict against the powerful ( +power) is to *be on the right side of history*. The very phrase "right (= correct) side of history" is also rooted in Marxist theory and jargon.

This model became the *criteria* for analyzing any economic and class-based situations (and eventually any and all aspects of society and culture). In such a model, there is always an oppressor (+power) and an oppressed (−power)— or a hammer and an anvil. The fact that this theory is based on certain "criteria" became the origin of the use of the coded term "critical" in this context. When the word "critical" is used, it is a coded reference to the use of these theoretical, *ideological*, criteria in the analysis. The term works all the more "magically" because it is hidden behind the more conventional use of the term, e.g. "critical thinking," meaning that certain objective or logical criteria are used to analyze a given situation. When ideology (or any set of philosophical presumptions) are used as criteria instead of actual logic, some unusual results become possible. Thinking in terms of ideological templates is perhaps another direct inheritance from the Christian Middle Ages.

So, as it all turns out, the theories of Marx had an effect less like a prophesy and more like a sorcerous incantation. Essentially, the Marxist model of history appears uncannily like that of Judeo-Christian tradition— only its causal agent has been revaluated from "God's Plan" to the "historical dialectic" or "historical materialism." In the Judeo-Christian model, there is an initial Edenic period, broken by man's transgression against God's law. This is followed by a long period of tribulation ended first by the incarnation of the Messiah who brings the program for salvation — the Evangelium — which is to be enacted by his earthly followers (the Church). Once this program has been spread world-wide, evil will be vanquished and a new paradise will be established on earth. The Christian version of this is, of course, highly spiritualized, and entirely dependent on the will and grace of God, while the Judaic version appears more materialistic, but just as reliant on the will of God. Man remains largely an impotent bystander in these models. The Marxist view similarly posits an early period of primitive communism, broken by the institution of the concept of private property (= Original Sin) and slave labor. This is followed by successive economic stages of feudalism and capitalism. The beginning of the end of the capitalistic phase is heralded by the revelation of Marxist theory as a program for "redemption." The essence of this new gospel is the theory of historical materialism and most importantly its structural mechanism known as the *historical dialectic*. This mechanism determines the progressive revolutionary movement in socio-economics from one sage to the next. The progression from the slave-state model to the capitalist model, for example, was illustrated in Marxist terms by the example of a major historical event in the 19th century: the American Civil War in which the capitalist system of the North prevailed over the slave-state system of the South. This historical transition is to be promoted and even enacted by socialist revolutionaries. Once revolution is has become global in its scope, capitalism will be vanquished and the classless, perfected Communist society will be established on earth. Parallels between Marxist and Christian and/or Judaic views of history have been posited by several scholars in the past. (See Riemer, *Karl Marx and Prophetic Politics*, p. 11-12) It is said that Marx was an excellent student in his school days in the subject of *religion*.

The political psychologist Wilfried Daim offered this diagram showing the model of Christian view of history:

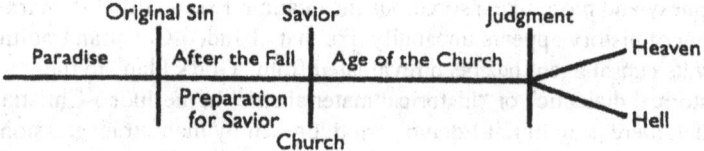

Daim (1958: 175)

Based on this idea, a similar model of the Marxist-Leninist view of historical development might be posited:

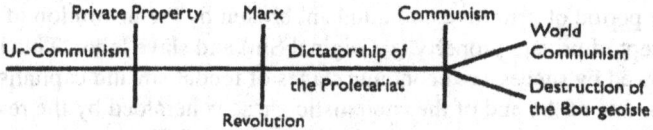

One might think that Marxist theory would have long since been discredited historically since political systems based upon it have consistently failed and generally instituted programs which were even more inefficient and intolerant than those the theory was designed to overthrow. The laboratory of history has shown how Marxism works when applied in practice, but it does not function in the way Marx envisioned it, or predicted it would work. Marxism has failed in the very theater of operation which it chose for itself: *history*. However, it is only as an *ideal* that Marxism has failed. Elements of Marxist thinking have definitely permeated deeply into popular political and academic culture in the form of such things as the previously mentioned notion of "political correctness." This formula of "political correctness" (even the connotations of the phrase) stems directly from Marxist orthodoxy which extended itself out from economic theory (Marx) into politics (Lenin) and then into the culture more broadly (through the Frankfurt School) and is based on the premise that there is an ongoing struggle by a variety of oppressed socio-economic groups who are at present viewed as being relatively powerless, e.g. women, African Americans, Hispanics, members of the LBGT community, the physically challenged, and so on. It is their collective aim (each group individually) to wrest socioeconomic power from those who are thought to possess it at present. This is based on the idea of "class struggle" as outlined by Marx, but applied to the culture more generally, and yet much more narrowly. The present strategy in the West is to create an aggregate of these sub-classes and to forge them together into a movement in which the actual interests of these groups are sacrificed to the common cause focused in the power possessed by a leadership class of professional politicians and activists— as Lenin designed the structure. Despite this, however, those groups are assured by Marxist theory of fighting the good fight, the moral fight, because the historical dialectic (or the Marxist "God," or at least one of them) is on their side. Hence to fight for their cause is to be on the "right side of history." Again, a concept drawn from Marxist theory. Their morality and their future victory is assured by the very fact that they are *currently* powerless, or can be made to feel so. This is why, for example, blacks cannot be considered "racists," or women "sexists," at least according to this theory based in the Marxist historical dialectic. This book should act as a warning to the various "client groups" that the Left has cobbled together for the present "struggle." The Old Bolsheviks too included many "alternative" types of people, all of whom were soon liquidated when they became inconvenient after power had been gained by the Party operatives.

So, to say that Marxism "failed" due to the historical fact that the Soviet Union failed is to miss the larger, more persistent, point of Bolshevism— which is as a program for the acquisition and perpetuation of political (and economic) power by and for a ruling elite belonging to a cadre of political operatives. In this regard, Marxism and Bolshevism by whatever name has proven to remain an effective tool because its practitioners have made themselves experts at identifying and exploiting the weaknesses of the established culture in order to undermine and eventually replace it.

## The Anarchy of Bakunin

Historically related to Bolshevism is the theory that came to be known as *Anarchy*. Bolshevism and Anarchy would seem have little in common theoretically, but historically and in terms of the kinds of people involved in, and attracted to, the two schools of intellectual rebellion against the *status quo*, they can be understood side-by-side. In his most famous work, the fragmentary *God and the State*, the Russian anarchist Mikail Bakunin at one point assesses humanity in terms of the Edenic myth and says: "[Satan] makes man ashamed of his bestial ignorance and obedience; he emancipates him, stamps upon his brow the seal of liberty and humanity, in urging him to disobey and eat of the fruit of knowledge."(Bakunin 1970: 10.) Bakunin saw humans as bestial creatures, but ones that were "endowed in a higher degree than the animals of any other species with two precious faculties— *the power to think and the desire to rebel*." Bakunin held that collectively and individually the development of man was characterized by three principles: *animality, thought* and *rebellion*.

Like most anarchists, Bakunin had his intellectual roots in Rousseau's idea of the "noble savage." It is seen that civilization and its institutions are the main evils in the world. It is determined that they cannot be reformed or altered, so they therefore must be destroyed so that the innate nobility of humanity may emerge as a matter of natural course once freed of all socially determined conventions. Bakunin followed de Sade in the theory that Man's great work was to *destroy*— Nature will then, as a matter of course, inevitably reconstruct a more perfect new dispensation.

Bakunin was not a systematic philosopher. He was an activist revolutionary, who said of himself: "I have no system, I am a seeker." He is said to have had a love for the mysterious and the irrational. This distinguished him from those he called doctrinaire communists, who

38

followed the systematic philosophy of Marx. Both of these philosophies are, however, based on a positivistic materialism. "God" was identified with the notion of "spirit," therefore the Devil, God's opposite and opponent, must be the equivalent of *matter*. Bakunin simplistically asserted that "intelligence" can be ascribed to matter due to its "dynamic nature and evolutionary quality." (Bakunin 1970: 12-13)

The ideas of Bakunin survived in the dark regions of the underground in the West. Such ideas continue to live on today among those who oppose any and all political authority. Obviously, the ideas of Marx have had a much more doctrinaire and institutionalized history. The fact that this historical development took place initially in still largely feudalistic, pre-industrial Russia and not in the highly advanced, modern and industrialized capitalist bastions of western Europe was a trend that Marx would not have appreciated. The fact rather disproved his theory of the particulars of the historical dialectic. It must be noted that the organization Bakunin tried to put together, the International, had already failed by 1876 due to lack of effective leadership. Imagine attempting to organize anarchists. Anarchism, however, continues to inspire new generations of anarchistic rebels, especially among the affluent and educated class living in the bosoms of Western democracies.

## The Narodniks

Marx was a German and his theories were created within, and with reference to, the heavily industrialized societies of Germany, France and England (as well as the northern parts of the United States). Russia was a very different sort of society— agrarian, highly religious and still close to its pagan past. The form of socialism that naturally grew its roots in Russia was something that was called Narodism or *Narodnichestvo* (народничество), variously translated as "populism" or "nationalism." The root word here, народ (*narod*) "people, folk," is semantically akin to the German *Volk*. The Narodnik Movement was decidedly nationalistic nd Slavophilic. The Narodniks opposed the rule of the Tsar and called for radical economic and political reforms which Tsar Alexander II opposed. He attempted to repress the Narodnik movement in the 1860s-1870s. The more he repressed them, the more radical they became.

The Narodniks viewed the peasantry, not industrial workers, as the revolutionary class. In many ways, they could be seen to follow in the footsteps of the agrarian revolutionary ideas of Thomas Jefferson. But the elite philosophical Narodniks were for the most part city-dwellers with a romantic vision of the rural peasantry. The misunderstanding of the peasants as they actually were led to general failure of the movement. The peasants were not ripe for revolution, were fanatically religious (in various ways) and loved the Tsar.

## People's Will

What can be characterized as "anarchy" was originally much more at home in the soul of Russia than was the eventual shape of Marxism. It appealed to the neo-pagan spirit of Russian Slavophilia. Originally linked to the Narodniks the movement known as the *Narodnaya Volya* ("People's Will") was organized in 1879 in order to undertake acts of terrorism in order to cause a peasant uprising and reforms. But the peasantry proved as ever stubborn in its loyalty to the Tsar. This organization became a network of intelligentsia focused on assassinating the Tsar. They succeeded on March 1, 1881 by killing Tsar Alexander II. The government reacted to this by rounding up and hanging most of the leadership of the "People's Will." The group soon became disorganized and lost its effectiveness. (Lachman 2020: 252 *et passim*)

## Occult Anarchy

The *Narodnaya Volya* clearly shows the roots of Russian Anarchism. The name we most closely associate with this movement in Russia is that of the aforementioned Mikail Bakunin. It should also be mentioned that Bakunin's connections to the occult were strong. He was himself a 33-degree Freemason. Freemasonry was, of course, a promoter of certain revolutionary ideas. Many people in those days, and perhaps even more today, indulged in dubious exercises in what have come to be called "conspiracy theories." Freemasonry was an institution in which individual men were brought into a brotherhood based on a common ideology. This brotherhood was one into which individuals of all nationalities entered and created a social link. In parallel to the structure of the order, Freemasonry can be seen to be an exponent of the contemporaneous trend in philosophy toward reason and rationality as a key to the solution to humankind's collective and individual problems. In many ways, Freemasonry mirrors the effects on culture that once upon a time the cult of Mithras exercised on the times of the late Roman Empire (100-400 CE) before the Christian Roman Church returned the region to a more irrational and totalitarian model.

Of course, anarchy would always be at a strategic disadvantage when confronted with organized opposition. Anarchy was designed to destroy order, but did not always have a good idea about what should replace that order which was being destroyed. The anarchistic trend was ever-present as undercurrents within post-Revolutionary Russian Leftists, such as Trotsky, Bogdanov and others. However, the attitude of Marx, and hence Lenin, might best be summed up in the statement by Marx that the idea of peasants (or even "common workers") being capable of effective collective action was the equivalent of the idea that "potatoes in a sack form a sack of potatoes." (Lagalisse 2019: 68) Anarchism is ideologically pure, but impractical. Marxism-Leninism proves to be effective but philosophically it is fatally flawed. Ultimately, Bolshevism overcomes all philosophical conundrums as it acknowledges within the ranks of its leadership that any talk of justice, freedom, equality and so on is merely a sorcerous *instrument* aimed toward the ultimate prize which is the seizure of political power and the means of production to be in the control of the inner circle of the Party elite.

## Russian Sects and Paganism

It has been noted that the Slavs in general, and the Russians in particular, have a special place in their national traditions for the Devil or devils. Russian popular religion on the very eve of the 1917 Revolution was still a synthesis of orthodoxy and rural demonology. The "dual faith" (Russian: *dvoeverie*) is a well-known phenomenon. This only goes to show how culturally conservative the typical Russian peasant was. The structure of this syncretic religion had remained virtually unchanged from the period of the conversion of the Russians to Orthodoxy nine centuries before.

In earlier centuries, Slavic and Balto-Slavic cultures were perhaps heavily influenced by the North Iranian steppe-tribes (e.g. Scythians, Sarmatians and Alans) from pre-history, but it may also be the case that the traits in question were proto-Slavic ones held in common with the Iranian branch of the Indo-European family of cultures. There were forces of light and ones of darkness that mirrored each other. A connection with the good deities helped strengthen the individual, while the dark ones might need to be appeased, and protection against them secured.

Right alongside of the peasants who believed in the magical power of saints (who embodied their old Slavic gods) and the powers of devils great and small, there was a variety of extraordinary sects or cults in late 19th and early 20th century Russia which thought of themselves as being "Christian" and which played an important role in history on the eve of the Bolshevik Revolution. Most of these sects rejected the spirituality of Russian Orthodoxy in favor of their own teachings. These were often steeped in Gnosticism and remarkably many of them held out the promise of the advent of some earthly paradise — a paradise in the here-and-now — as opposed to the more orthodox assurance of a heavenly one. Some of these sects were even ideologically rationalistic and materialistic. They prophesied a time when mankind as a collective body would become god-like. Sects such as the Raskolnik, the Molokans, Duchohorzis, Stundists, Neo-Stundists, the Nyemolyaki (non-prayers), Medalyshchiki and Nyeplatelshchiki (non-tax-payers) and some others taught about the evils of private property and of the Russian Orthodox Church. They stood for the universal brotherhood of humanity, the coming advent of an earthly paradise characterized as the true form of *Christianity*.

In addition to these there were more extreme sects in Russia at this time that included the Khlysti ("whippers") and the Skoptsi ("mutilated," i.e. "castrated") who were an offshoot from the Khlysti. The Khlysti were libertines who practiced a form of mysticism involving flagellation and sexual orgies. The reference to "whipping" in their name may be a distortion of their own self-designation *Khristy*, "Christians." Their rituals, called *randniya*, could often turn into sexual orgies accompanied by flagellation. The religious function of these was thought to be that repentance is best done after the commission of grievous sins: "Sin in order that you may obtain forgiveness." There were tens of thousands of members of this sect, organized in cells called "Arks" headed by a male and female pair called the "Christ" and "Mother of God" respectively.

Out of the Khlysti grew the Skoptsi (скопцы) "castrates," in the 1760s. This sect practiced extreme asceticism and corporeal mortification. This included the mutilation of the sexual organs and amputation of limbs. The name was, of course, not their self-designation. They called themselves "The White Doves." Historically, the leaders of this sect were typically believed to be the reincarnation of Christ— and sometimes the Czar would indulge their ideations and crucify them on the Kremlin wall! Some people see similarities between these sects and Gnostic cults of the late Antique period. These sects do compare very favorably with tendencies present in Gnostic cults from the first few centuries of the Common Era. (Walker, 1983: 183-184). But it is more likely that the traits are survivals of the dualistic features of the ancient Slavic and North Iranian tribes.

It is estimated that on the eve of the Bolshevik Revolution there were approximately 100,000 Skoptsy in Russia. The Soviets attempted to eradicate them and put many of them on trial in 1929. Although they were indeed almost eliminated over the decades there are said to be remnants of them even in the 21st century in Latvia and in the Caucasus.

The presence of these extremist sects, and especially that of the Skoptsy, appears to be a clear sign of a certain collective mass hysteria and pathology in the Russian populace. These are clear indications of the self-destructive tendencies on a mass scale which helped pave the way for what happened in the early part of the 20th century and helps to explain why the people had such a long-standing tolerance for the abuse heaped on them in the Stalinist years. Self-destructive tendencies are often a sign of coming calamities.

The famous rogue holy-man, Grigori Y. Rasputin, may have been influenced to some degree by the teachings and practices of the Khlysti— at least in spirit. However, hard and more reliable evidence points to him being a rather naive, simple peasant in most of his outlook on life. His own writings support this view. The image of Rasputin that has come down to us in popular history is the result of propaganda mounted against him by enemies of the Tsar. Certainly, he was no devil-worshipper. This despite the fact that he is listed as one of the major influences on Anton LaVey on the dedication page of his *Satanic Bible* and despite the persistent popular image of him as some sort of Satanist. Frequently it is found that the mythic *image* of a man in history greatly exceeds, and/or is something profoundly different from, any factual data about him. The generation of the 1960s was probably decisively influenced by the Hammer "horror" film entitled *Rasputin— the Mad Monk*, starring Christopher Lee!

The final and perhaps most important, if apparently most invisible, ingredient to the mixture of elements at the foundation of esoteric Bolshevism is that of the Russian native faith (*Rodnovery*) which was ever present, usually unacknowledged by most members of the educated classes of Russia, but nevertheless understood to exist in the Russian soul. Somehow the native faith of the pre-Christian Slavs had survived in the folkways of the Russian people, obviously most strongly in the countryside. Russian and Pan-Slavic Romantics of the 18th and 19th centuries acknowledged the existence of this phenomenon, and saw that it was preserved in the folk-religion parallel to Russian Orthodoxy, especially among the so-called Old Believers.

Whereas in the Germanic world there was a halting movement toward the revival or reawakening of the ancient, pre-Christian native culture and religion(3) among Slavic poets and intellectuals there was the persistent and widespread belief that the old ways had never died out among the peasantry and that they remained and remain very near the surface of Slavic cultures everywhere.

I will return to discuss the topic of the Rodnovers in contemporary Slavic culture in chapter 6.

## Science

Nowhere in history since the Italian Renaissance had what is generally thought of as "science" and what is usually considered some sort of "occultism" been so closely intertwined than they were in the late 19th and early 20th century in Russia. The reason for this seems in both cases to be similar. Technology and hard scientific advances were being made, but the general culture was still deeply connected with the myths and mores of ancient tradition.

From the time of the establishment of the Russian Academy of Science in St. Petersburg in 1725 by the Tsar Peter the Great, under the advice and through the inspiration of the German philosopher and scientist Gottfried Leibniz, Russian advancement in the sciences was broad and innovative. An enormous amount of scientific, technological and medical innovations and inventions can be found to have been contributed by scientists from the Russian Empire and subsequently the Soviet Union. Not all of these were Russian in the strictest sense, as both the Tsarist Empire and the USSR were very much multi-national states wherein Poles, Baltics, Ukrainians, Georgians, and so on, were subjects or citizens of the state. Such technological innovations range from the electric powered train (1874) and electric transformers (1882) to the radio (1885) to the helicopter (1912) and dozens and dozens more. Often such inventions and breakthroughs were only put into actual production in other countries, but both the Empire and the USSR were hotbeds of scientific innovation, both theoretical and practical.

It was only natural that a culture so steeped in religious faith and folk-religion would often turn its scientific energy to questions having to do with those things usually addressed by religion and even magic.

It seems clear that Russian Bolshevism can be seen to have its deep roots in two sources: Marxism and the Russian avant-garde of the Silver Age, which included elements of Russian Cosmism. The first is well-known, established and has diverse schools debating various kinds of orthodoxy. The second is only something that has become visible as a set of related ideas in more recent years, but that does not mean that it was not a true body of thought which was even more deeply ingrained in the Russian psyche than Marxism ever was. The intellectual tide of Revolution the Bolsheviks rode to power in 1917 floated on waves made up of the Cosmist ideology swirling with the undertow of Silver Age Decadence. These all provided the occult roots of what became Bolshevism.

Russia was very much open to ideas imported from foreign lands, especially France and Germany, and occult concepts would later become extremely conspicuous in this regard. Theosophy might be considered a Russian construct, as it was formulated by the Russian expatriate Helena Petrovna Blavatsky. An off-shoot of it was Anthroposophy shaped by Rudolf Steiner, which was also imported with some influence in Russia.

The eventual ideological battles waged between and among Marxist, Bolshevik and Socialist philosophers took on much of the same motives and strategies that characterize medieval arguments over theological points surrounding such obscure concepts as "the Trinity," "Original Sin," or transubstantiation. The aim is usually always the same in such arguments: to get the better of one's opponents and gain their power for one's self. Discovery of the *Truth* rarely seems to be the objective. Ideology was weaponized as a form of sorcery.

# 2. Before Lenin Came: The Russian Silver Age

Valery Bryusov

Throughout Europe the decade just prior to the beginning of the 20th century and leading up to the First World War was a time of great cultural dynamism. In Russia, this time period is referred to as the Silver Age (ca. 1890-1914). This was a time when the Russian avant-garde artists, poets, and performers indulged in free love, drugs, and occultism. There were many figures who demonstrated various eccentricities. The alternative cultural world of Russia at this time was very receptive to foreign influences from France, Germany and the Anglo-American world. Literary models such as Poe and Baudelaire along with the philosophy of Nietzsche were inspirational to a wave of spiritual rebels who can be characterized as Decadents and Symbolists. But through the influence of Fedorov and his students, ideas of Futurism were also strong. In every regard, Russians made these influences into something that was in the end uniquely *Russian*.

An important presentation of the Russian Silver Age, including the present-day reflections of its ideologies in Putin's Russia, is offered by Gary Lachman in his book *The Return of Holy Russia* (Inner Traditions, 2020).

The dominant philosophy of art was for a period that of Symbolism, which theoretically is rooted in the work of Charles Baudelaire and based on an idea he expressed in his poem "Correspondences" in *Les Fleurs du Mal*. In his 1886 Symbolist Manifesto the French Symbolist theoretician, Jean Moreas, defined the artist's work in the school of Symbolism as: "The Symbolist poet attempts to express a 'primordial idea,' not in itself, but through concrete phenomena which were in fact appearances with 'esoteric affinities' to it."

Russia was awash with the most eccentric characters imaginable. Although ideas were imported freely from abroad, it must also be remembered that Russia produced her share of occult teachers on her own— Blavatsky, Gurdjieff, Ouspensky as well as the Nicholas and Helene Roehrich.

Symbolist artists were especially open to the influences of the occult and to engaging in behaviors designed to evoke occult ideas in the populace. Natalya Goncharova (1881-1962) was a Futurist and pioneer of the style known as Rayonism. She was known to sometimes dress in men's clothes and lived out of wedlock with fellow artist Larionov. Also, her nude life studies were thought to be too explicit, especially to have been created by a woman. She was actually brought to trial on charges of pornography. For these reasons, perhaps she and Larionov immigrated to France in 1914. She made herself notorious with shocking public behaviors. Both Goncharova and Larionov painted hieroglyphics and flowers on their faces and then would promenade down the street— but Goncharova also sometimes went topless with symbols painted across her breasts.

Valery Bryusov (1873-1924) was a poet, prose writer, dramatist, translator, critic and historian. The fact that he was a major member of the Russian Symbolist movement and was known to practice black magic, conduct séances and engage in other activities typical of the Decadent school all make it seem unusual that when most of his friends in the *avant-garde* fled Russia after 1917, he actually stayed and participated in the Bolshevik Revolution. In his younger days he had seduced followers, addicted them to cocaine and enticed them to suicide. These same skills he later put in the service of the Revolution. Also, in his younger days he translated works by Poe, Verlaine, Maeterlinck and Mallarmé and was under the influence of Fedorov and Tsiolkovsky. As time went on, Bryusov lost some of his prestige in the literary world and after the Revolution he fully cooperated with the Bolshevik government and held a position in the cultural ministry.

Another fascinating figure of this time period was an ingenious composer named Alexander Nikolayevich Scriabin (1872-1915) who invented an "optoelectronic machine" able to convert into sound any symbol or sign drawn on a large pane of glass. Visible signs were thus converted into audible sounds. Other modes of such "sonic alchemy" were also pursued whereby colors could be keyed to sound as well. Scriabin operated in a theoretical world shaped by Theosophy and Nietzsche. He planned to perform his great composition: *Mysterium* in the Himalayas, but he died before this dream could be fulfilled. In the 1930s there was a resurgence of interest in his ideas and a Soviet engineer named Yevgeny Murzin secretly constructed a synthesizer based on Scriabin's designs, which he called the "ANS Synthesizer" in honor of Scriabin's name by using his initials. Murzin had to work in secret because this was the period of Stalinist purges. The machine would only be completed and put into operation in the 1950s. It is used in the composition of the electronic music soundtrack for Andrei Tarkovsky's Soviet-era science-fiction film *Solaris* (1972). Strange and experimental musical inventions were a general part of early 20$^{th}$ century Russian culture. We are also reminded of the invention of the Theremin, an electronic musical instrument by Léon Theremin (= Lev Sergeyevich Termen) [1896-1993]. This translates movements of the human body into sound.

Certainly, one of the most important Silver Age thinkers and writers was Vladimir Sergeyevich Solovyov (1853-1900). His surname is also frequently transliterated as Soloviev. He was born into an educated and reasonably prosperous family, and by his teenage years he embraced nihilism and formally rejected the Orthodox Church. Over time he would mellow his views and try to synthesize and reconcile his ideas with those of the established faith. His way of spiritual synthesis made use of Greek philosophy, Gnosticism, Buddhism and the Jewish Kabbalah. His philosophical efforts always strove for a bringing together of different religions: Roman Catholicism and the Eastern Orthodox, as well as that of the Christians and Jews. Soloviev was an activist within the Society for the Promotion of Culture among the Jews of Russia (1863-1929), and even spoke Hebrew himself. This was a learned society meant to aid Jews in the process of emancipation and "enlightenment."

On the other hand, especially toward the end of his life, Soloviev developed a deep distrust of, and animosity toward, the cultures of the Far East— principally China and Japan. He rejected Buddhism as nihilistic and feared a coming conflict with "Pan-Mongolism." Russia did engage in war with Japan five years after his death, the Russo-Japanese War (1904-1905), a war in which Russia was defeated.

One of Soloviev's most important works was *The Crisis of Western Philosophy: Against the Positivists* in which he attacked the dominant positivistic philosophy that was sweeping through the intelligentsia of his day, and embraced the perennial concepts first expressed by the ancient Greeks, such as Plato, whereby the key lies in the development of noetic comprehension by which an insight is developed which integrates the apprehension of both the phenomenon (validated through dianoia) and the noumenon, which must be sensed by intuition alone. Here the essence of an object can only be sensed noetically, which presupposes and integrates both logic (science) and intuition.

It can be seen why Soloviev had such a significant influence on Russian Symbolists with his syncretic view of religion and spirituality. Both his work and his personality were influential on Dostoevsky and Leo Tolstoy as well. He was driven by the concept of Sophia, "wisdom," as a figure of the divine feminine providing unity and mercy. She could be compared to the Hebrew concept of the Shekinah, "the *presence* of God." As regards the community of his fellow men, he promoted the Russian concept of *sobornost*. This is a term which describes a community of people who give up individual benefit for the sake of the well-being of the whole community. This can be meaningfully compared to the concept of fraternity, in which the individual does gain immediate benefit from his association with others. It can be seen how this mystical concept could lie at the root of the attitude toward community and the individual found in Soviet times, when the individual was supposed to subordinate his benefit for the whole community. Another related concept which he introduced was "syzygy" which denotes "close union."

It is somewhat ironic that Soloviev was a recluse who never married or had children. He often lived alone and would work deep into the night. In this night, he intuited a world beyond the senses.

## The Esoteric: From the Satanic to the Cosmic

### The Satanic Underground

It is widely speculated upon as to just how much "Satanic" activity was taking place in Silver Age Russia. Individuals, especially artists of various kinds, seem to have enthusiastically embraced the image and meaning of Satan in their work, and in their lives. This world is generally introduced by

Kristi Goberg's article "The Shade of Lucifer's Dark Wing" (1997) and it frequently discussed by Gary Lachman in his *The Return of Holy Russia* (Inner Traditions, 2020).

For the most part the most visible exponents of Satan were poets such as Aleksander Dobroliubov, Konstantin Balmont, Andrei Bely and Valery Briusov, whom we have already met. The fact that the worship of Satan in any "organized" or open way appears to be hard to find might well be taken as a sign of just how serious these Russians took their activities. There were legal and religious reasons to keep such activities strictly secret, and they were approached in a deadly serious manner by all concerned.

First of all, Satan was seen as a Miltonian hero of rebellion against oppression. These poets were what are referred to as aesthetes, who were for the most part well-to-do and well-educated individuals motivated to experience the extremes in life. They read Goethe, Poe, Baudelaire and Nietzsche and their hero, besides Satan himself, was Mephistopheles. They indulged in drugs of all kinds, experimented with alternative sexualities and were as often as not (at least for periods of their lives) bent on self-destruction.

A man such as Briusov styled himself as a *chernomag* (черномаг) as a "black magician." But in the end, this did not stop some of them from making the transition into the Bolshevik world, when the time came. The essentially *artistic* tenor of this world is rather reminiscent of the way in which the American magus, Anton LaVey, artistically recreated himself in the very image of the Devil in the late 1960s. Satan seems to rise up in turbulent times.

Into this heady mix of Satanism and the occult, much of it imported into Russia from abroad, there suddenly appeared (in the winter of 1904) a Russian "holy man," a *strannik*, as they are called, who was highly charismatic and apparently gifted as a confidant and healer. This was the previously mentioned Grigori Yefimovich Rasputin. He held no position in the Russian Orthodox Church and had been illiterate until a brief educational stint as a young adult at a monastery where he finally learned to read and write. Rasputin was born a peasant in the village of Pokrovskoye and most of the things that have been said about him have been shown to be fabrications. He entered the world of the salons of the rich and royal and made the acquaintance of the Tsar and his family. Rasputin was able to be effective in treating the hemophilia of the Tsar's son, Alexei, with his spiritual healing methods. His influence at court was deeply resented, and a variety of rumors were spread about his negative influence on the royal family. The legend of Rasputin was engendered during his lifetime and only grew more outlandish after his assassination by Prince Felix Yusupov, who provided a personal account of the murder which only further enhanced Rasputin's reputation as a sort of superman, i.e. that he was impervious to poison and had to be shot several times to kill him and that even when he was thrown into the Malaya Nevka River he was apparently still alive and attempting to rise up again. It may be true that he did survive one gunshot that should have been fatal and fought back against his assassin. Yusupov's embellished account was apparently motivated by an attempt to show just how *powerful* and *malevolent* the holy man was, thus demonstrating just how "heroic" the assassination should be seen to be. In any event, the Rasputin episode was just another in the pre-Revolution occult mania that was sweeping Russia and paving the way for an extreme solution to Russia's problems.

It is noteworthy that Anton LaVey published a ritual focused on the imagined diabolical image of Rasputin— again no doubt inspired by the aforementioned Hammer Film *Rasputin the Mad Monk*. The ritual is called "Homage to Tchort" and appears in his anthology of rituals book called *The Satanic Rituals* (Avon, 1972). The rite was supposedly informed by a member of his church who was a former Russian Orthodox believer. In any event, the performance of such rituals is designed to place the celebrant in the mood of the times, within that excessive Russian Silver Age where Satan was seen as a rebellious hero of the time to come.

Andrei Bely was the pen-name of one Boris Nikolaevich Bugaev (1880-1934) who was one of the leading poets of the Silver Age and who also became a proponent of a modified form of the Anthroposophy of Rudolf Steiner. Earlier in his life he was influenced by the ideas of Soloviev, with whose family Andrei was acquainted. He spent time in Germany, Switzerland as well as in Russia. Bely worked on synthesizing the ideas of Soloviev and those of Steiner and came to extol the idea of the "Eternal Feminine" (ultimately derived from the poetry of the great German man of letters, Johann Wolfgang von Goethe, specifically from the latter's *Faust* (Part II). The Eternal Feminine is identified with the "world soul," or more particularly with the idea of a supra-individual ego. This is an ego-consciousness that is actually shared collectively among all individuals. At first Bely was an acolyte of Briussov, but the two became embroiled in a lovers' triangle with Nina Petrovskaya— which became the background for Briussov's masterpiece *The Fiery Angel*. This novel tells the story of a 16th-century German scholar who tries to win the love of a young woman whose spiritual life has been seriously compromised by her dealings with occultism and demonic forces. She is therefore seriously undermined by her participation in these occult practices and her dealings with unclean forces. The story became the basis of Sergei Prokokiev's opera of the same name. When the Revolution did eventually come in 1917, Bely supported the Bolsheviks and even served on the Organizational Committee of the Union of Soviet Writers.

One of the most intriguing characters from this world of the Silver Age was Alexander Dobrolyubov (1876-1945). He was a Symbolist poet, but was best known for his lifestyle and image rather than his actual literary works. He burst upon the scene when he was only seventeen years old and earned the attention of Briussov. Gary Lachman writes of Dobrolyubov: "He wore only black, including fur-lined gloves that he never removed, smoked opium and was thrown out of school for preaching suicide to his classmates, with some success." (Lachman 2020: 282) He eventually left the windowless chamber in which he lived, with its black walls adorned with Satanic imagery and went out into the world to become a prophet of Satan. He began to wear iron hoops around his body and gathered a certain following for his ideas.

In their own ways, these Silver Age aesthetes, Symbolists and nihilists prepared the way for more widespread extremes in the years which followed their time of flourishing in the late 19th and early 20th centuries. These individuals can also to some extent be seen as "canaries in the coal mine," as many of them met with self-destructive ends in a sort of magical prefiguration of the ultimate fate of the *Zeitgeist* itself. The avant-garde in Russia was made up of a relatively small group with great influence in the culture. Russia was, and is, a country with a large population, which the Bolsheviks will exploit in war-strategies later, but until recently Russia has been marked by an elite and restricted intellectual world, in contrast to the situations found in Germany, England or France.

## The Esoteric and Cosmic

In the Russian Empire, during the years just prior to the First World War and the Bolshevik Revolution, two men were developing esoteric teachings that would affect the world for generations to come. These were the Russian Peter Ouspensky and his one-time teacher the Greek-Armenian G. I. Gurdjieff. An amazing fact about Gurdjieff is that he spoke many languages, five of them fluently: Armenian, Greek, Persian, Turkish and Russian. He composed in Russian and some say he *thought* in Persian. He was generally educated in Russian, and spent most of his early years in some part of the Russian Empire. Ouspensky was a dedicated anti-Bolshevik. This stemmed directly from his personal and intimate experiences with the abusive violence of the Bolsheviks which he experienced personally at the time of the Revolution and in its aftermath. He said of it: "Persons inclined to abstract thinking persist in seeing in Bolshevism not what it actually is, but what it ought to be according to their theoretical deductions."(Webb 1980, p. 169) Because neither of these teachers appears to have had any sympathies with the Bolshevik cause, and their ideas seem to have had little influence on philosophers within that movement, we will spend little time with them here. In both cases, they can be seen as sparks emitted from the Russian Empire who could not be reconciled with Bolshevik thought.

Russian Cosmism is an eclectic nexus of thought encompassing various aspects of religion, philosophy and science concerned with the origins of things as well as their use in a process of human evolution toward an ideal state of being— both immortal and reasonable. Cosmism drew from Theosophy (Eastern and Western Esotericism), Marxism as well as from the Russian Orthodox Church. Essentially Cosmism in its early phases could be said to possess three main tenets:

Immortality

Emergence

Actualization

Immortality is to be achieved, as a *physical* reality, either through rejuvenating of the blood (at one point they thought of the possibility of transfusions from younger people to older ones) or even the resurrection of the dead by scientific means. In *emergence* humans will break the confines of the natural world encompassing both space and time. In *actualization* Cosmists commonly promoted a concept called "active evolution" which in part held that humans of the past would actually evolve into humans of the future, in a future in which they will possess unlimited powers. It was thought that a group of evolved individuals would develop a moral and ethical utopia in the future.

# Konstantin Tsiolkovsky

## Tsiolkovsky 1934

Konstantin Eduardovich Tsiolkovsky (1857–1935), was a school-teacher of physics and mathematics in the provincial town of Kaluga ninety miles southwest of Moscow. He was nearly deaf. And he is also considered to be the "grandfather" of eventual Soviet space exploration. This honor is rooted in his bold conceptualization of the practical aspects of space-travel using liquid-propellant rockets, space-stations and means of humans surviving space travel in spaceships. His ideas were all worked out and published well before the time of the Revolution. He even illustrated his ideas in an educational science fiction story in 1893 entitled *On the Moon*. Since the world's technologies had not yet begun to approach the content of his visions of future possibilities, many of his ideas have to be classified as being virtually "occult" for the time he formulated them. But despite the fact that he held many unusual, or even *occult*, ideas upon which his theories were built, he was eventually hailed by the official Soviet state as a hero and was given high honors and a pension. All this was in itself remarkable for a shy and retiring soul in the savage world of post-Revolutionary and Stalinist Russia.

In 1903 Tsiolkovsky published a book entitled *The Exploration of Cosmic Space by Means of Reactive Devices [Rockets]*, which is considered by historians of space-travel to be the first actual scientific work on the topic. It was Tsiolkovsky's belief that by colonizing space humanity would make great leaps toward perfecting itself— becoming both immortal and happy.

Tsiolkovsky was actually a supporter of the Bolshevik Revolution, but the results of that event created a system in which he was not particularly adept. In an effort to promote science and technology he was made a member of the Socialist Academy in 1918, but he continued to work on as a high school teacher of mathematics until he retired in 1920. It would only be toward the end of his life that Tsiolkovsky garnered much attention among state officials and therefore from the general Soviet public.

Tsiolkovsky supported the idea of eugenics from a purely scientific viewpoint, but because of the prominent role this idea played among the German Nazis, this was an unpopular idea in the Soviet Union. From the middle of the 1920s forward the importance of his other work connected with space exploration was increasingly acknowledged. The state both honored him and provided some financial support for his researches. He was especially popularized by two Soviet writers, Yako Perlman and Nikolai Rynin between 1931 and 1932.

Many of Tsiolkovsky's ideas were reluctantly dismissed as being "impractical" even by his admirers in Russia. But German rocket scientists such as Wernher von Braun did pay close attention. Allied investigators at the Nazi rocket research facility at Peenemünde discovered a translation of Tsiolkovsky's works on rocketry and it is reported that it was glossed on every page with notes and comments in von Braun's hand.

As young men Valentin Glushko and Sergey Korolev, who were leading figures in Soviet technology related to the possibilities of space travel, had studied the ideas of Tsiolkovsky and dreamed of making his fantastic visions emerge into actual practice. At first Korelev set his sights on achieving a landing on Mars— probably originally inspired by the fictional/philosophical work of Bogdanov. This Martian dream probably set the Soviet program back because it was over-ambitious and it was not until 1964 that they abandoned the dream of a Marian landing and began to compete directly with the US in the race for the Moon.

Tsiolkovsky wrote a book entitled *The Will of the Universe: The Unknown Intelligence* which was published in 1928. In this book, he outlined a philosophy with many points of contact with panpsychism— that intelligence is omnipresent in the universe. It is now considered to be an essential work of Russian Cosmist Philosophy. He dreamed of the day when humans would colonize the outer reaches of space. Although Tsiolkovsky did not believe in traditional religious cosmology, he did hold that a cosmic being did govern humans, manipulating them as "marionettes, mechanical puppets, machines, movie characters." In so doing he did adhere to an at least quasi-orthodox Marxist mechanical view of the universe. This universe, he believed would one day, in the distant future, be controlled through the power of science and industry.

Tsiolkovsky died in Kaluga on September 9, 1935 after an operation for stomach cancer. In his will, he donated his life's work to the Soviet state.

## Political Dimensions

Russia in this Silver Age was not only an elite world of Symbolists and Futurists, of course. The age was one politically and socially marked by upheaval and discontent among the Russian people. The time period was one dominated by the reign of Tsar Nicholas II (1884-1917). The country was only slowly industrializing, at a pace far behind that of England, Germany or France. There was, nevertheless, significant urbanization with a rise in population in the cities due to an influx of workers from the countryside. These workers were relatively more powerful than in the West due to the fact that the industry in Russia was mainly owned and run by the state, or by foreign companies. The larger factories employed a huge amount of the work-force— due in part to the inefficiency of the mechanization process. Such circumstances allowed workers and peasants to form political parties, since state and middleclass interests were weak-willed. As economic conditions worsened in the 1890s and early 1900s, the political pot began to simmer.

In general, the domestic political policy of the Tsar was to repress the middleclass and any groups that might develop on the political Left. Political parties of all kinds sprung up all over the country and littered the land with the blossoms of discontent. The first signs that the pot might boil over were the widespread workers' uprisings that broke out in 1905. These were quelled with promises of economic and political reform. Few of these reforms materialized as the bad working conditions, poor living circumstances and widespread hunger lingered on.

The pot containing its witches' brew of military and political incompetence, workers' discontent and raging radical political parties— including the recently formed Russian Social Democratic Labor Party — finally boiled over with the impending defeat of Russia in the First World War by the Germans. By February 1917 the Tsar's government collapsed and Lenin awaited his moment to take command of the nation.

# 3. The Age of Lenin

## The Occult Lenin

Vladimir Ilyich Lenin (1870-1924) founded the Bolshevik (majority members) faction of the Russian Social-Democratic Workers' party in London in 1903. This wing opposed the Menshevik (minority members) faction. Lenin, born Ulyanov, became a Marxist revolutionary after the execution of his brother who was implicated in a plot to assassinate the Tsar. Lenin was later arrested and sent to Siberia in 1895. In 1900, he fled to western Europe to organize socialism internationally. Then, in 1905 he returned to Russia to participate in the abortive revolution of that year, but fled back to Europe again in 1907.

Lenin is most often viewed as a purely "political" figure, which is probably the best way to view his impact upon the world. However, as most times, there is more to the story than mere appearances.

He lived in exile mainly in Switzerland in the interim. While there he made many contacts with occultists and esotericists, both from the West (France, Germany, Austria) and his native Russia. Among those he met was the infamous Jörg Lanz von Liebenfels, one of the most eccentric writers of all time, but who had some points of contact ideologically with certain Russian Cosmists.

Lenin returned to Russia after the outbreak of the 1917 revolution in March of that year. He was escorted and given safe passage in a sealed train from Switzerland to St. Petersburg by German officials who correctly believed Lenin would finish the Revolution and thus take the Russians out of the Great War. Lenin accomplished his mission. He led the Bolshevik overthrow of the provisional government in November. This was still in October according to the old style Russian calendar, hence the importance of that month's name in Soviet historical symbology. As chairman of the Council of People's Commissars Lenin became the virtual dictator of Russia. From that time to his death in 1924 Lenin worked to establish the professional revolutionaries of the Bolshevik Party as the ruling elite of the country, while suppressing all internal opposition to himself and working to spread Communist revolution world-wide. One of his closest associates, and heir apparent, was the one-time seminary student, thug and bank-robber, Joseph Stalin.

Lenin's opponents often envisioned him as the Antichrist— but so did many of his supporters! Certainly, he attempted to style himself as an "apocalyptic" figure who attempted to transform a whole culture in a very short period of time. His successes can be ascribed to his mystical vision of a primitive culture transformed into an ultra-modern, electrified and totally efficient *machine*. To Lenin this machine was what others might call god.

Every individual human being — worker or peasant — is essentially a machine, and so the collective aggregate of all workers and peasants form a larger machine— *the* machine. As Lenin saw it, his inner task was to make the whole machine work as efficiently, perfectly as possible, under his direction and control. Ultimately, the machine would be made perfect. This is why science and technology were virtually sanctified in Soviet Russia. This analysis of man as a machine, of course, is historically derived from the French philosopher Julien Offray de la Mettrie, but there are also other more Russian connections. Gurdjieff famously maintained that men are machines, and that only by realizing this, and undergoing development can the individual cease to be a mere machine and become a true man, in the positive image of God. However, for all intents and purposes as a rule, man remains a machine.

The New Man, the New Machine — the *Homo Sovieticus* — would be created from the scientific communist programs of the Bolsheviks. Clearly this ideology is drawn from the Cosmism of the Russian Futurists and Symbolists. These programs were indeed set into motion by the Party. Such activities involved the dismantlement of Orthodox religion to be replaced by the new science of Communism. As any good Communist would have told you, no Communist state as yet exists. No one has yet attained this goal. As we have seen, before Communism — a world without laws, government, property or even a Party — is possible, years of Socialism are necessary.

As regards Lenin and the occult, there is a curious deep-level aspect to this. The Ulyanov family tradition held that Vladimir's great-grandmother was executed as a witch by the authority of the Russian Orthodox Church. His connection to her and the traditions which she seemed to instill in the family was this: that miracles are possible, that anything is feasible, no matter how unlikely it might seem to others. In other words, what Lenin was practicing was always a form of witchcraft or magic. In his own mind, without this component, his task of Revolution in 1917 could never have been completed.

But, of course, the first miracle, that of taking over the government of the Empire of Russia by his organization was the easier of two miracles which had to be performed. The second was maintaining control and giving direction to the controlling Party and masses of the Russian people. Most, both inside and outside Russia, were banking on him not being able to do this, but he prevailed.

People today popularly call the philosophy that has swept into elite circles in the West "Marxism," but it is really more Leninism than

Marxism. Marx provided a basic theory, but it took Lenin to make this into a political technology for the acquisition and maintenance of *power*. Marx may have supplied a sort of mathematical theory, but Lenin put this into action and proved its effectiveness in the theater of history. It will be noted throughout these historical discussions that the actual protagonists of the Revolution are thinkers and philosophers, not workers, peasants, soldiers or students. But it is essential for the system to work that the thinkers convince their client populations that the Revolution is *for them*. These clients have to be portrayed in propaganda as innocent victims of tyrannical violence and oppression, and that only the vision provided by the intelligentsia can save them from their ongoing plight. But from the standpoint of the Party these clients are merely expendable means to the ultimate end, which is the acquisition and maintenance of power by the ruling Party elite. This brilliant stroke of genius by Lenin is the model used by subsequent revolutionaries from Hitler to Mao and from Castro to all competitors in politics (whether at the office, in academic departments or electoral politics in Western "democracies"). Whether this dynamic is at work in your own present environment can be judged by the imbalances in power one can see. For example, in Western academics, power is now focused on the administration and a *very few* tenured professors— menial tasks (such as teaching classes and sitting in those classes while paying ever increasing fees) are handled by the rank and file on the collective farm.

All of this is a testimony to the continuing power of the philosophical spell cast by Vladimir Lenin.

## V. D. Bonch-Bruyevich

Vladimir Dmitriyevich Bonch-Bruyevich (1873-1955) was Lenin's personal secretary and expert on sects and religions for the Bolsheviks. He was an early revolutionary and was arrested for participation in a student demonstration and exiled to Kursk. He became a part of the same group Lenin was in around 1895 and in 1896 left for Switzerland to help organize socialism internationally as an activist in the *Iskra* circle. *Iskra*, which means "spark," was a socialist newspaper that acted as a clearing house for socialist organizations.

Bonch-Bruyevich had a special interest in the dissenting religious sects in Russia. As we have seen these groups were persecuted by both the Tsarist government and the Russian Orthodox Church. It was the belief of Bonch-Bruyevich that such sects could be aids in developing and spreading revolutionary propaganda and ideology. He once interviewed Rasputin and assessed his religious views as being Orthodox, and that he was not a proponent of any of the radical sects, such as the libertine Khlysti. Bonch-Bruyevich studied, lived with the Doukhobors, a heretical ethnic sect from southern Russia, and even travelled with a group of them to Canada when they immigrated there in 1899.

In the political and Revolutionary realm, Bonch-Bruyevich was a devoted aide to Lenin, he ran business affairs, was an enthusiastic proponent of Bolshevik ideas and handled all sorts of matters having to do with publishing, printing, and so on. In 1918, he was elected to be a member of the Socialist Academy of Social Sciences. He worked on or founded many of the early and enduring Party organs: *Pravda*, *Izvestya*, and others. He even established a Party archive. His talents and abilities were maximized by Lenin.

After Lenin's death, he was an active writer on the topic of Soviet history, religion, sects, atheism and literature. His best-known work is a sort of "official" biography of Lenin. Since Bonch-Bruyevich served as secretary to Lenin in the years right after the revolution he was in an ideal position to write such a work. He was the director of the State Literary Museum in Moscow beginning in 1933 and also director of the Museum of the History of Religion and Atheism, and the Academy of Sciences of the USSR in Leningrad (St. Petersburg) between 1946 and 1953.

## The Rites and Rituals of Early Bolshevism

Our best, most invaluable and most convenient source for the early cultural history of Soviet Russia is Fulop-Miller's *Mind and Face of Bolshevism* (1927). In this book, which first appeared in German, it is clearly shown that the early Bolsheviks had an extremely radical "plan," implicit in the Marxist-Leninist philosophy, for the transformation of the human species into a collective god-like machine. In many respects this was a more practicalized version of the vision of earlier Cosmicists. But *how* was this to be done in practical terms? A good deal of this plan was up to the head of the People's Commissariat for Education (Narkompros), one Anatoly Lunacharsky, about whom more later. All vestiges of the old system, the bourgeois society and culture, had to be destroyed utterly. As institutions, the church and state could be eradicated or controlled in a relatively easy manner— through brute force. But the psychological and cultural (collective psychological) hold of the old ways which had been imprinted on the minds of humans by centuries of conditioning, would require a second phase: the institution of new cultural and quasi-religious forms to replace the old ones.

It might be easier to understand the magical aspects of National Socialist mass gatherings, due to the fact that they tended to be highly choreographed with uniformed individuals moving in disciplined unison. The platforms for such Nazi rites tended to be a defined space: the Zeppelin Field, the convention hall, etc. However, the Bolshevik rites were very different. They appeared to be undisciplined, mass gatherings in the streets with the participants appearing in amorphous crowds. This is not to say that the Bolshevik political ritual was without definite ceremonial patterns and organized elements of behavior. The contrast with the Nazi rallies is all the more jarring due to the fact that the Bolshevik style of "street demonstration" was adopted by the Left in the West and remains a familiar feature of political liturgy in contemporary life. These rallies usually have a beginning point (A) and a definite (often meaningful) route, the masses move along the street carrying signs and banners with messages on them, chants are performed until point B is reached. There a representative gives a speech or proclamation of aims and purposes, songs are often sung and finally the crowd disperses (with or without some violent confrontation). We are used to seeing such ceremonies, so much so, that they don't seem like *rituals* at all anymore. They are designed to appear to be spontaneous outpourings of the collective will, but in reality are always well-planned and organized events.

That the old-style Bolshevik May Day demonstration seemed to descend into a primitive state of one-mindedness of a mass psychology is not without ideological Marxist content. Did not Marx theorize that society had originally been a Communist state, without laws, private property, borders, and so on? Is not the cosmic aim and purpose of Revolutionary ideology to help society return to the Communist state? That being the case, certain early Bolshevik political rituals were designed to give the participants a sort of temporary foretaste of what that Communist paradise would be like.

That erudite writer on topics relating to early 20th century Russia, René Fulop-Miller commented in his insightful and contemporaneous *The Mind and Face of Bolshevism* (1927):

> ...[I]n Russia the Marxian theory of social evolution was apprehended from the beginning as the practical demonstration of a doctrine of salvation. According to Karl Marx, Engels and the modern Socialists, society is gradually to advance from its primitive "anarchical" economic forms, first by the inevitable road through a concentrated form of capitalism to more and more rational methods of organization, and finally to universal collectivism of work and production. But this which Marx and his disciples

regarded merely as a gradual process of evolution, the Bolsheviks wished to turn forthwith into a concrete thing, a new and vital being. For once they had mastered the idea of collectivism they wished straightaway to have an infallible material proof of it, the physical manifestation of the conception. The historic and economic process of evolution in the direction of collectivism was, as it were, in an instant transformed by Bolshevism into a spiritualist "phenomenon of materialization," into the million –footed monster apprehensible by the senses, the "mass-man."

This impatient desire for a materially apprehensible manifestation of spiritual things is shared by the Russian Bolshevists with the disciples of that other faith which is so primitive and materialist in tendency, and to which they are deeply akin in many other points as well, with spiritualism. It is easy to recognize in the peculiarly banal, dogmatic instructions for the artificial creation of the Bolshevist collective man, a ritual analogous to that of the "séances." The "spirit circle" of Bolshevism is "party organization", the "séance" in which the "collective presence" is corporeally manifest becomes the street demonstrations, and finally the formulas for raising the spirits are: "Left! Left!" "Bash their heads in!" or "Historic materialism." And when all the magical conditions for the Bolshevist séance have been created, there appears, growing out of the circle, the phenomenon of the collective monster, who remains for a period among those who have conjured it up; it breathes, moves, and lives for the duration of the demonstration.

(Fulop-Milller, 1927: 17)

The huge icon-like images of men such as Marx, Engels and Lenin (and later Stalin) were thought of by the people in ways similar to the manner in which Russian Orthodox icons were thought of. They were not mere portraits or representations but rather talismanic images which had the power to influence the world.

In the efforts of the first phase, the Communist youth organizations, especially the Komsomol-League, were instrumental. There were massive campaigns to criticize, lampoon and debunk the Russian Orthodox Church, Judaism and Islam along with every cultural dimension of these religions. The public was rationally "re-educated" against belief in icons or the miraculous powers of relics of the saints. In the former effort, for example, comic versions of icons were produced in magazines such as *Bezbozhnik* ("The Atheist"), an example of which is reproduced below.

Comic Icon from the Cover of *Bezbozhnik*

What came to be called "Red Masses" were held in the old churches. These lampooned the Orthodox faith with comic mockeries of their ceremonies. Churches were turned into museums of atheism and the hammer and sickle replaced the saltire cross atop the spires. Belief in the curative powers of the miraculously preserved bodies of saints was debunked with rational and scientific explanations of how the bodies were preserved by artificial means. It may appear ironic, but consistent with the nature of cultural continuity, that Lenin's body was preserved the way it was— as a miraculous example of "Soviet Sainthood." But the shocking truth is that it was not meant ironically that Lenin's body is so preserved. Actually, this preservation served two purposes which I will discuss momentarily.

After the Bolshevik Revolution, some Soviets occasionally thought about the creation of a replacement for the "opiate of the masses." They did not wish to create a new religion to exist alongside of the secular authority, simply because ideologically this duality was rejected. There was only one true order of the universe and it was defined by materialism and historical materialism was its cosmic plan. But the negative campaign against religion in general could only take them so far in transforming the society. Certain rites and customs were created in the time of Lenin to act as positive answers to the human need for such things. There were rites for "baptism," marriage and funeral.

One of the most interesting of these is that of the baptism, or naming of a newly born "comrade." Names given to children were sometimes selected by collective action in the factory or within party offices. A whole new typology of names surfaced in Russia. These were intended to reflect Revolutionary values, e.g. Revolutia or Oktyabrina (in honor of the "October" revolution) for girls and things such as Rem (an acronym for the Russian phrase for "Revolutionary Electrification Program") for boys. The naming was done as part of a "Red Baptism" presided over by local Party secretaries in Party facilities. Usually children were named in group ceremonies. The meeting hall was draped in red, the gathered workers sang "The International" — which had become the "hymn" of international Communism — and the parents swore to bring up the child as a good Communist. The official naming was done ceremonially with the words:

> We the undersigned herewith confirm that into the
> union of the Socialist Soviet Republics a new
> citizen _____ (here the first and last
> names are inserted) has been received. As it is
> that we give to you your name in honor of
> _____ (here an explanation of the
> socialist significance of the first name is
> given), we greet you as a future worker and
> founder of Communist society. May the ideals of
> Communism henceforth form the content of your
> long-lasting life! May you become one of those who
> will lead the great task of the proletariat to its
> conclusion! You shall step beneath the red flag!
> Long live the new revolutionary citizen!
>
> (Fulop-Miller 1927: 258-259)

The Soviets naturally concluded that the new, younger generation would be the true transformers of humanity. Instrumental in this process for the transformation of the species would be a new sexual morality. Until the advent of Stalinism there was a Red sexual revolution following in the wake of the political revolution. Both marriage and divorce were made easier— with no involvement with ecclesiastical sacraments. Abortions were also easily available, but not encouraged. Certain aspects of the new

Red sexuality suggest possible links with the old Khlysti sect— at least in spirit.

In the pages of the official newspaper *Pravda* there appeared an article on this new morality pertaining especially to the young members of the Komsomol by a female ideologue known only as Smidovich. She reasoned that the more primitive ("animalistic") the rules of conduct for sexual life are, the more *Communistic* they are. She insisted that the youth should not place any restrictions on their sexuality. No female should refuse the sexual advances of a male member of the Komsomol, for example. In the Komsomol itself orgies, called "African Nights," were organized in which there were approximately 70 percent men and 30 percent women. (Fulop-Miller 1927: 265-266) This type of early alternative activity did not survive long after the introduction of Stalinist protocols.

These radical alternative approaches to various aspects of human life and culture in general did not last for very long. Once, it seems, that the advantages gained by the state by instilling chaos in the culture had been established, a quick return to repressive, even puritanical, values were (re-)instituted. This is a typical pattern for the establishment of tyrannical regimes.

> Following the October Revolution, the materialist nature of Fedorov's theories appealed to many in the new Soviet state, and his universe-scale ambition did not seem out of place in a radicalized society that had abruptly overcome such seemingly intractable obstacles as private property. While it never became a part of official Soviet doctrine, much of cosmism dovetails with the ethos of early post-revolutionary utopian socialism in its drive towards a classless, egalitarian society completely dedicated to the emancipation and self-transformation of humanity, and to the construction of a man-made paradise on earth. The first post-revolutionary decade saw an explosion of cosmist ideas and their application in very diverse areas of life, from art and science to the practical organization of labor, time management, and the health system. This period also sees the emergence of biocosmism—an atheist, anarchist-infused variant of cosmism strongly influenced by futurism in poetry and art. At a certain moment in the mid-1920s, it is in fact difficult to find a creative thinker in the USSR who is not influenced by this set of ideas. However, by the early 1930s, much like most other intellectual movements that differed from the "scientific Marxism" embraced by Stalin's government, cosmism becomes a subject to be purged, along with its protagonists and practitioners—most of whom end up in jail, in labor camps, or in front of firing squads.
>
> From the Editorial to *E-Flux Journal* #88

In theory, Marxism-Leninism, informed by Russian Cosmism, assumes a possible perfection (deification) and even immortalization of humanity *as a species*. But such perfection is only possible on a collective basis, not an individualized one. The nature of this collective is determined by materialistic/economic criteria and the process of perfection is governed by a transpersonal force in history. That the human can become (a) god essentially appears to be akin to what some might call a "left-hand path" premise, but that the process by which this occurs is *collective* and *not willed* (but inevitable) would take the ideology out of any ultimate consideration as a left-hand path system. The modifications made to the cosmological theories of Marxism made by Lenin not only made the system more practical and workable, but also steered it more in the direction of what can be called a left-hand path ideology. Plato or Pythagoras might have told Marx that any deification must be based on *individuality*. Clearly the original Cosmist ideology of Fedorov was far more idealistic and actually democratic than any form of pure Marxism-Leninism.

"Collective perfection" is an idea that is not unique to Marxism-Leninism. It is, of course, found in Judaism in which the people await salvation and perfection by a Messiah. This idea was borrowed into Judaism from Zoroastrian thought where it is theoretically closer to the Bolshevik concept— since all of humanity is included, not just a "chosen folk group." It should be noted, however, that the concept of an elect *group* of humans who will gain knowledge, power and immortality is something that enters into institutionalized Christianity (where anyone can become a member of the select group through membership in the cult). So, a similar concept is promoted in "political" ideologies such as Marxism or National Socialism. The former is more akin to the Christian model, as it depends upon mutable characteristics (class, conviction, knowledge and dedication) whereas in the case of the latter the characteristic is supposedly immutable and biological. Such ideologies are generally dependent on *linear* models of history— the group as a whole must progress through time until the advent of collective perfection (or "salvation"). For the National Socialist or Jew (from whom the Nazis derived the idea) the collective is deified in terms of an *ethnic* group. For the Marxist or Christian, the collective is determined on a more voluntary, ethical, or economic basis. But it is also somehow "predestined" or determined. In the one instance by the historical dialectic and in the other by "God's Plan," or "God's Grace."

# Anatoly Lunacharsky
# and God-Building

## Anatoly Lunacharsky

Anatoly Lunacharsky (1875–1933) was a Freemason, Symbolist writer and dedicated Marxist. He was also one of Lenin's closest co-conspirators. Lenin appointed Lunacharsky as thehear of the People's Commissariat for Education (Narkompros) Narkompros in 1917. This made him the "Commissar of Enlightenment" and put him in charge of planning all education, propaganda, publishing, theater, films, museums and even street festivals. Lunacharsky was an avid student of comparative mythology and the occult and the main designer of the project known to the Bolsheviks as "God-Building." Essential to this project was the destruction of all of the old gods and religions (Christian, Buddhist, or whatever) and constructing a new way of thinking based on Marxist principles alone. He wrote what is referred to as a "God-Building" play called *Vasilisa the Wise* which is about Mitra— a secular Messiah. Mitra or Mithra is, of course, the name of the Indo-Iranian god of law and justice.

Lunacharsky was a complex man. Not only was he one of the Old Bolsheviks, he was also a serious Symbolist author and a devotee of the occult. To the outside observer, he appeared to be a gentle professorial type. His fellow Bolsheviks saw him as "gentle hearted." But in point of fact he feigned the persona which enabled him to be at the center of a web-work of ruthless revolutionary operatives and artists and poets of all sorts. So, Lunacharsky may have appeared to be kind, but he was at the nexus of a ring of some of the most vicious professional revolutionaries of the twentieth century — he was friends with refined artists and brutal killers, and understood the role of each.

At one point Lunacharsky was allied with the Vperedist faction of the Bolshevik Party, along with his brother-in-law, Alexander Bogdanov. As they developed, Lunacharsky's radical ideas on religion were in stark contrast to the official Soviet ideology in the USSR. These hard-liners wanted religion, and anything like it, simply to disappear from human life. Their form of "atheism" amounted to a simple and radical rejection of the idea that anything existed apart from the measurable phenomena of material existence. Lunacharsky's ideas on God-Building were later adopted by other Soviet leaders on a private, virtually secret, basis.

In 1926, and following, the Russian-Soviet writer and medical doctor, V. Veresaev advocated the development of aesthetically pleasing and standardized rituals for important moments in the lives of individuals, such as giving names to infants, weddings and funerals. Although it might be said that the state already had certain rituals, e.g. the annual May Day Parade, he characterized them as lacking in inspiration. He and other thinkers noted that people continued trying to go to church because of the poor quality of anything the Soviets offered as a replacement for religious expression. But as might be expected, Veresaev, was attacked by official Soviet apparatchiks and so his ideas, like those of Lunacharsky, were ultimately officially rejected.

## God-Building
### богостроительство

From a technical occult perspective, the idea of "god-building" is linked to the practice of constructing what are called egregores or *imagospurii*. In this process, an image is used (most often a unique and special one) to become the focus of individual or (most especially) collective energy and imagination which "feeds" the object or image. It then takes on a life of its own and can become in turn a source of energy and power to those who actually themselves created the "god." This practice is tantamount to an occult charging of a battery and use of the stored energy for various purposes. Such a process is constantly at work in the use of icons and images of gods, demons, or whatever.

Here, as in so many other places, the Bolsheviks took inspiration from a German thinker. In this case, Ludwig (von) Feuerbach (1804-1872), who envisioned a "religion of humanity." Feuerbach wrote a highly influential critique of Christianity in 1841 entitled *The Essence of Christianity*. This work affected other thinkers such as Darwin, Marx, Engels, Freud, Wagner and Nietzsche. He was a student of Hegel in Berlin, and is seen by some to be the link between Hegel and Marx. Feuerbach was an advocate of atheism

71

and materialism, but did so in an imaginative manner which ascribed a significant role to human creativity and to the power of the human mind.

Feuerbach's ideas were to some extent rooted in the "cult of reason" found during the French Revolution. This idea was taken up by some of the early Bolsheviks and promoted as the idea of "god-building." These strategists thought that instead of abolishing religion and cult altogether, that they should replace it with new gods, new myths, rituals and symbolism to fill that space in the human experience. Such rituals, myths and symbols would be utilized in a meta-religious, or magical way according to their psychological and social effects. These forces would be harnessed for the purposes of promoting the cause of the Revolution and Communism. So, a new god would be built making use of these tools in a magical way. What Lunacharsky proposed was the development of a new religious feeling and practice that was totally rooted in science, with no "supernatural" elements. Old rituals would be re-interpreted and new ones created. These ideas were mostly expressed in his two-volume work *Religion and Socialism* (1908–11). There he proposed the bold theory of *bogostroitel'stvo* (богостроительство, "God-Building"). He held that scientific socialism is actually the most *religious* of all religions, and so the Social Democrat is the most deeply religious of all.

In Lunacharsky's theory, established and orthodox religion was seen as being false and was used by the state and capitalists as a tool or weapon for the oppression and exploitation of the people. However, the best way to overcome this was not by denying the religious urge in humanity altogether, but by re-directing it to a positive and revolutionary model. The basic idea held by Lunacharsky was one generally followed by certain ideologues in the National Socialist movement in Germany just a few years later as well.

In the thoughts and philosophy of Lunacharsky we clearly see the battleground that still exists in culture between the religiously minded (who believe that God alone has the power and sets the right standards of human life) and the humanists, or "secular humanists," as they are sometimes called. The latter are of the opinion that human reason, correctly understood and used, should be the only arbiter of truth and meaning in life. Of course, Marxists can be considered the ultimate in secular humanists, but only if we, with Marx, see man as a simple *economic* machine. Men such as Lunacharsky, and all of the other more Cosmically minded thinkers of Russia saw humanity as having more than just mere economic value. Lunacharsky foresaw the problems with the reduction of humanity below its actual value, and tried to account for this in the Soviet plan. He was, of course, ignored, much to the final peril of the USSR.

His criticism of Marxism as such was that it was too mechanical and deterministic to ever be an effective philosophy capable of generating any amount of enthusiasm among the masses. Clearly, Lunacharsky was not of the opinion that "man is a machine." Emotion and morality are important to the human species, and will persist regardless of education. If orthodox religion is weakened, other features will fill in the 'spaces" in the human mind where these patterns exist. This could be planned, or go unplanned and unexploited, which would be a waste of an opportunity to deepen the Socialist message.

In his landmark 1908 work *Religion and Socialism* Lunacharsky asserted the following points:

1. Socialism is fighting against religious superstitions and prejudices based on empirical knowledge of objective and subjective science.
2. Socialism is fighting against the religious intellectuals serving the bourgeoisie, just as with the secular intellectuals supporting the bourgeoisie.
3. Socialism is alien to militant atheism, based on opposing prejudice and violence against people.
4. Socialist freedom also implies freedom of religion and an independent search for the truth for every person.
5. Socialism cannot dogmatically hold any one position on the statements "God is" or "There is no God", and takes a position of agnosticism or "open possibilities".
6. Socialism unites secular and religious ideological groups in the struggle for the proletariat. Any action aiming to merge socialism with religious fanaticism, or militant atheism, are actions aimed at splitting the proletarian class and have the formula of "divide and rule", which plays into the hands of bourgeois dictatorship.

Feuerbach's original concept of a "religion of humanity" posited that God is to be replaced by humanity itself as an object of worship. This initially meant that single individuals, heroes, if you will, would not be so worshipped. Rather the idea was to "deify" the *collective* essence of humanity and place it in the stead of God. The achievements — both actual and potential — of humanity would optimally be the object of such attention. In the end, of course, the technology of inventing a "new religion" fell away from the philosophical intentions of men such as Lunacharsky and was applied in the creation of a cult of personality focused on the supreme leader (i.e., Stalin). This same process has occurred in other Communist states historically— Mao, Fidel, the Kims, etc.

A variety of other German philosophers were his inspiration in the original views surrounding "god-building.' Besides Feuerbach, these included Richard Avenarius, Ernst Mach and Friedrich Nietzsche.

Lunacharsky himself also had a particular interest in the mystery schools of ancient Greece, especially the Eleusinian Mysteries held in ancient times at the PanHellenic Sanctuary at Eleusis. Structurally, these could be used as a model for modern communal ritualism and become a way of imparting moral (i.e. "political") concepts in an effective manner.

Those focused on the God-Building project understood the term "religion" to indicate the common connection among all individuals, and individuals and communities— now, in the past and into the future. Lunacharsky himself considered that humans, in a truly socialistic system, must merge into an organic unity, and that as such the atheistic philosophy could not achieve this end, as its sterile essence was not equipped for such a heroic task. In Lunacharsky's system humanity itself is seen as the transcendent entity, and thus the object of the worship and even love of individuals.

Lunacharsky correctly, but "heretically" from a Leninist viewpoint, identified the religious aspects of the philosophy of Marx. As we have noted, this would include an irrational faith in the mysteries of the historical dialectic, the inevitable victory of socialism and its belief that science and material existence accounted for all human relations.

Lunacharsky, following the general line of positivist thinking so prevalent in Europe at the time, denied the divinity of Christ, but he revalorized and re-interpreted him as a revolutionary and even saw him as the "world's first Communist." All of this is very reminiscent of the German positivistic re-interpreters of Jesus (e.g. the "German-Christians") who posited a racially pure "Aryan Christ." The history of Christianity is heavily laden with such re-formulations of Jesus in the image (physical or ideological) of whatever was fashionable at the time. Certainly, Lunacharsky had to change the way he wrote about Christ over time, as the fashions and ideological details "evolved" in the course of the Soviet state.

In the new religion envisioned by Lunacharsky there would be prayers to and for "progress," "humanity," and "human genius." In keeping with the symbolism of the collective, such prayers would be performed in groups as a collective activity, rather than by individuals. The liturgy of this new religion would be performed in new sorts of temples — theaters where plays would be performed to inspire the masses and act as teaching tools for psychological and sociological revolutionary change.

Despite Lunacharsky's position in the Party and relationship with Lenin his ideas about God-Building were forcefully rejected by Lenin himself. He saw that such an approach might compromise the strictly atheistic stance of Marxism. Much of his objection seemed based on the past historical abuses of the Russian Church and he did not want to give any quarter to what he called reactionary forces. Lenin clearly saw how religion had been used as a tool for oppressive governments throughout history. Beside these arguments, Lenin also leaned on the authority of the earlier rejection by Karl Marx of the ideas of Ludwig Feuerbach about a "religion of humanity." The ironic and odd thing about this orthodox Bolshevik assessment of religion is that Communism asked for the same sacrifices, but did not promise a better future life for those making the sacrifices today. Many of the more radical Cosmists had answers to this conundrum, of course. The only member of this faction who seemed to go uncriticized was Bogdanov.

Lunacharsky's new religion was to be a religion of humanity and science, and to be free of any "super-natural" beliefs. But, as we see in various discussions in this book, the Cosmists in general could conceive of things just as apparently fantastic as any ancient mystic without theoretically resorting to the supernatural. The posited hidden — or *occult* —dimensions of nature would be quite sufficient to enable humanity to achieve what had formerly been accounted for only in the miracles of the church or in the magic of sorcerers.

This God-Building faction of early Bolshevism would urge the creation of a new religion based on a synthesis of folk-religion and socialism. In the 19th century among Slavic Romantics and intellectuals it was widely accepted that pre-Christian elements had survived among the peasantry and that the state or condition of *dvoeverie* ("double faith"), common enough in the Middle Ages throughout Europe, was alive and well in places like Russia and Poland. Among those who were interested in this phenomenon, and who were also Revolutionaries of one kind or another, from Narodniks to Socialists, were Alexander Herzen, Kikolay Ogarey and Mikael Bakunin. Early Bolsheviks such as Vladimir Bonch-Bruyevich, Maxim Gorky, Vladimir Barzarov, Anatoly Lunacharsky and Alexander Bogdanov were also involved in one way or another with this idea.

The Bolsheviks of V. I. Lenin stepped upon the stage of Russian history amidst a mixture of widespread popular pagan survivals and demonology, with sects preaching the advent of "heaven on earth" and other cults practicing extreme forms of libertinage and asceticism. These sects and occult movements form a deep background for a culture ready to believe in, and act upon, extremely radical ideas.

It is seen that Bolshevism attacked Russian culture with a double-edged weapon— with the sickle of reason as well as the hammer of the irrational. It is a disarming form of propaganda to present a populace with a mystical, occult, irrational idea (Marxism) and preface the introduction with the assertion that it is a "purely scientific" and "mathematically correct" analysis of history and an equally methodical approach to what must be done to transform the world into a "heaven on earth." But in order for the irrational and mystical side of things to be accepted, and the extreme forms of cultural asceticism to be endured by the majority of the people there must be a cultural matrix of the irrational to act as a foundation. This Russia had— and still has. Such a circumstance is a powerful and energetic tool for cultural transformation, but it must be handled wisely— which rarely happens in history.

So, ultimately Lunacharsky's idea of God-Building was officially not pursued, but the magical "technology" of the idea was obviously applied in Soviet statecraft. The idea was then philosophically revived among Russian philosophers in the 1960s.

## Alexander Bogdanov

Alexander Bogdanov

Alexander Aleksandrovich Bogdanov (1873-1928) was born Alexander Malinovsky in what is now Poland and is one of the most interesting of the early Bolsheviks. He was a physician, philosopher, revolutionary and science fiction writer. He attended Moscow University, but was arrested and exiled because he joined a prohibited student group, so he had to study at the remote University of Kharkov, from which he graduated in the school of medicine. In the 1890s he began to write theoretical works on economics. At the same time, he began to study the works of Lenin, and was arrested and exiled once more.

Bogdanov became a leading figure in the early phase of the RSDLP in its Bolshevik faction, which he co-founded with Lenin. The two leaders interacted in Geneva and in Kokkola, Finland. Bogdanov was arrested and exiled, but spent much of his exile outside Russia. He published a philosophical study in three volumes between 1904 and 1906 entitled *Empiriomonizm* [Empiriomonism] in which he attempted to synthesize the thoughts and theories of the German philosophers and scientists Karl Marx, Ernst Mach, Wilhelm Ostwald and Richard Avenarius. Bogdanov's ideas were influential on many early Bolsheviks, and his intellect repeatedly bought him into competition with Lenin as the chief ideologue of the movement.

Clearly, Bogdanov could qualify as a real "renaissance man" among Russian Revolutionaries as a physician, scientist, science fiction writer, philosopher— and he helped organize bank robberies with Lenin and Stalin, e.g. the robbery of the Tiflis bank in 1907! A couple of years later he was contesting Lenin for leadership of the Bolshevik faction. Each had their supporters, but Lenin went on a campaign of destroying Bogdanov's reputation as a philosopher by accusing him of "philosophical idealism." This came in the form of a book Lenin wrote entitled *Materialism and Empiriocriticism* (1909). This was one of the several sorts of "heresy" a Bolshevik could find himself accused of. Bogdanov was then expelled from the Bolshevik faction by a vote held at a conference in Paris.

He joined with his brother-in-law, Anatoly Lunacharsky, along with Maxim Gorky and others who belonged the Vperedist faction. *Vpered*, Russian for "forward," was a sub-faction within the Bolshevik wing, notable as a faction generally critical of Lenin. Bogdanov, Lunacharsky and others set up the Capri Party School on the island of Capri in 1910, which then moved to Bologna in Italy. At approximately this same time Lenin set up the Longjumeau Party School outside Paris. These were think-tanks aimed at fomenting revolutionary activity in Russia.

Eventually, due to his intellectual rivalry with Lenin, Bogdanov was expelled from the faction in 1909. He generally retired from overt political activity in the years prior to the Revolution of 1917. But would play a part in the government ultimately formed by the Bolsheviks, for although he remained a critic of Lenin and the doctrinaire Bolsheviks from their political *left*, the prestige of his intellectual work and his position of seniority in the movement protected him from any sort of serious persecution.

1912 Bogdanov abandoned his revolutionary activities altogether and returned to Russia in 1914— just in time to be drafted into the army at the outbreak of WWI. He served as a doctor in the Second Army. This Army was almost entirely wiped out, either killed or taken prisoner, in the disastrous Battle of Tannenberg in August of 1914, but luckily Bogdanov had been dispatched to Moscow to accompany a wounded officer and avoided the calamity. He continued to serve in the front line of battle and eventually fell victim to the nervous disorder then called "shell-shock." From then on, he served at an evacuation hospital. He continued to write economic articles analyzing the situation in Russia at the time. It was his prediction that after the war state-capitalism would replace finance-capitalism.

By the time of the actual Revolution in 1917 Bogdanov was not a part of the organized Party at all and remained a non-partisan philosopher and agitator. As the Russian Front and the Russian state itself were collapsing, he disapproved of the continuation of hostilities with the Germans and advocated the establishment of an inclusive socialist government. Bogdanov openly criticized the Bolsheviks and Lenin on the basis that they had embraced a misguided "leadership principle."

In all of this Bogdanov can be seen as almost unique in his level of internal criticism as regards the leadership within the Socialist movement— especially unique in that he survived liquidation. He noted that organizations, once they have gained power, tend to attempt to recreate society in the image of the organization. This never left room for the development of a wide variety and diversity of heroic individuals, once the collective stamp had been applied under the cult of the leader.

In Bogdanov's analysis, the Bolsheviks became too militarized in their approach to all problems due to the fact that so many soldiers joined the Party during and immediately after WWI. The militaristic mentality made it more difficult to solve problems, due to a disparity between the system and the nature of the problems it was assigned to solve.

After the Revolution, Bogdanov was given several offers to rejoin the Party, but he continued to refuse. He became a professor of economics at the University of Moscow in 1918 and the director of the Socialist Academy of Social Sciences.

# The Proletkult

In a bold effort to overthrow the old "bourgeois culture" in order to replace it with a new "proletarian culture" (= *Proletkult*) Bogdanov organized a movement to this end between 1918 and 1920. This was a Revolutionary action aimed at the construction of a new future through re-education. The Moscow Proletarian University was founded and the movement received financial aid from the Bolshevik government, as did many experimental programs during this time. But because of the intellectual diversity and comprehensive vision of leaders such as Bogdanov, the Bolshevik leadership became suspicious. In 1920, the Prolekult was denounced as being "petit bourgeois" and a nest of "socially alien elements." Essentially Bogdanov was expelled from the Bolshevik hierarchy because of his criticisms of it and his formations of groups to compete with it.

The Proletkult itself was directly influenced by Cosmist ideas. Such concepts were at the center of works by writers such as Mikhail Gerasimov and Vladimir Kirillov whose poetry was characterized by sweeping words of praise for the physical labor, machines, technology and the collective body of the workers who are seen to be launched from the bonds of Earth to colonize planet after planet.

One of the perennial interests of Cosmism was, of course immortality, or at least rejuvenation. Bogdanov, who suffered from eye-ailments, began a series of blood transfusion experiments in 1924. He also founded the Institute for Haemotology and Blood Transfusions. Even Lenin's sister, Maria Ulyanova, participated in experiments at the institute for the promotion of health and rejuvenation. Bogdanov was treated for his eye problems and after eleven sessions appeared to be rejuvenating. But things went badly when he was transfused with the blood of a young student who suffered from malaria and tuberculosis.

An analysis of Bogdanov's earlier writings, both fictional and philosophical, show that he envisioned a future technocratic society. Through artificial systems he thought, human leadership and the corruption and inefficiency that comes along with it, could be avoided. Since the Bolshevik hierarchy was really only interested in theories that maintained their own power, Bogdanov was always "suspect." Many of Bogdanov's theories and ideas have proven to be prescient with regard to recent developments in the industrialized world.

During the Stalinist era Bogdanov became a hero to some underground dissidents who supported the Revolution, but who wished to develop beyond the autocratic political order.

As noted, Bogdanov published works of fiction as well as philosophy. Both were influential, but his fiction works really struck a deep chord in the Russian psyche. His science-fiction masterpiece was a novel entitled *Red Star* published in 1908. It told about a modern-day (1908) Russian being transported to the planet Mars, where he witnessed the functioning of a communist utopia. He uses the text to show how communism could work, but does not shy away from what he sees as possible looming problems in the future. It contains predictions about future technology, social structures and gender issues. For example, he predicted that the two sexes would become more similar to one another as communism advanced. There would be sexual liberation for women, as well. Bogdanov went into some detail in the novel about the practice and use of blood transfusions on Mars. This mirrored his own obsession with the idea, one that eventually cost him his life.

In his follow-up novel Bogdanov wrote a prequel in 1913, entitled *Engineer Menni*. This went into the "history" of how Mars became a communist society. Of course, it was his view of how Russia might attain this goal as well.

Bogdanov's most cosmic philosophical work was incorporated and published in his three-volume study entitled *Tectology: Universal Organization Science* (1913-1929). Bogdanov's visionary concept of *Tectology* foreshadowed ideas that later became known as "Systems Analysis" and Cybernetics. He ascribed much of the inspiration for his thinking on these concepts to the German philosopher Ludwig Noiré (1829-1889). It was Bogdanov's aim to unify all the sciences — social, biological and mechanical — within one monistic framework. Bogdanov's three volume work was given a German translation in 1926, and it was probably the inspiration for later scientists such as Norbert Wiener. So, later Soviet skepticism surrounding the idea of Cybernetics, a skepticism which set back Soviet advancement for decades, might have had its original root here. Both Lenin and Stalin came to regard Bogdanov's theories as personal threats to their power-base in dialectic materialism, and again Tectology, like much of Cosmism was only re-developed in Russia in the 1970s.

# Gleb Boky
## and
## The Search for the Red Shambhala

## Gleb Ivanovich Boky

The most important investigator of the possibilities of Shambhala in Central Asia was Gleb Ivanovich Boky (1879–1937) who was an ethnic Ukrainian, early supporter of the Bolshevik cause, a leading member of the Cheka (Soviet secret police), ruthless organizer of the early Soviet system of concentration camps— and an enthusiastic investigator of the paranormal. Boky was one of the Old Bolsheviks, but his most conspicuous efforts in the occult dimension was during the Stalinist phase, which was also the time when he himself was phased out.

Boky was born in the Ukraine, but educated in St. Petersburg, where he graduated from the Mining Institute in 1896. He had already been radicalized in his student days, and had become a dedicated professional revolutionary for the RSDLP by around 1900. He spent time exiled in Siberia for his subversive efforts on behalf of Lenin's Bolshevik faction. He was elected to positions within the Party and fought actively in the 1905 Revolution. He was arrested many times and sent to Siberia two more times.

From early on Boky was an expert in cryptography, which was important in the days when the Socialists organized covertly in underground cells which had to communicate with one another secretly. Later his cryptographical skills were not only found to be valuable in encoding secret messages, but he also was a master of decoding foreign codes, and the Soviets were historically able to do this far better than their counterparts in the West.

He took the Party-names "Kuzma," "Diadia" and "Maksim Ivanovich." With the success of the October Revolution in 1917 Boky allied himself with the "Left Communists" headed at the time by Nikolai Bukharin, who later drifted to the "right." Boky became an operative in the developing secret police apparatus, the Cheka and then the NKVD, and was an active participant in the Red Terror during the time of the Civil War between the Reds and Whites.

It seems likely that Boky was eventually psychologically disturbed by the role he played in instigating and attempting to manage this Red Terror, and that this disillusionment led him to delve ever deeper into esoteric studies from about 1920 onward in order to try to find a way out. His thin physique (he suffered from tuberculosis contracted in prison) and aristocratic bearing made him an oddball among his colleagues. Despite any private doubts he might have had, he remained a dedicated leader in the Soviet system of the courts and secret police.

He arranged for presentations of paranormal activity by G. I. Gurdjieff and P. D. Ouspensky in the laboratories of the secret police at one point. Boky also had a significant bohemian side. He arranged for what have been called "children of the sun" outings at his country-side *dacha*. These were nude sun-bathing parties that usually ended in drunken orgies, in good Russian tradition. It has always been a hallmark of Russian culture that "sex scandals" in the British, American or even German sense are unknown.

As a long-time student of Theosophical concepts Boky was interested in the esoteric avenues to the perfection of humanity. In consultation with some Mongol lamas and his friend Alexander Barchenko he contemplated an expedition in the 1920s to discover Shambhala, the hidden subterranean city of esoteric Tibetan tradition. Barchenko was a respected biologist and researcher into the paranormal, who would eventually be executed as part of Stalin's Great Purge in the spring of 1938. Boky endeavored to bring together the doctrines of Kalachakra Tantrism and those of Marxist-Leninism. In this endeavor Boky and his friend Barchenko undertook experiments in a secret laboratory under the control of the NKVD which made use of some Buddhist techniques directed toward the discovery of a way to develop the perfect Communist human being— the new *Homo Sovieticus*. The actual expedition to Central Asia never occurred, although one under the rival Soviet Foreign Commissariat did occur in 1924. His hoped-for mission to Central Asia to find Shambhala was to be undertaken in the expectation of finding a secret power nexus to help the Soviets conquer the world.

He continued his work for the political police and is thought by some to have been an architect of the Soviet Gulag system, which was a form of internal exile and labor camps for prisoners of all kinds, including those suspected of "political crimes." In most ways, these were merely an extension of the system used in Tsarist times.

At least one faction within the NKVD secretly opposed to Boky concocted various stories about him in a secret dossier which accused him of various bizarre crimes, including the idea that he was really a vampire who drank human blood. This type of story was told about him from the beginning, but only when Stalin became suspicious did the stories become a problem. He was then suddenly arrested in May of 1937, "tried" on November 15th, sentenced to death and shot the same day. At the time of the "Thaw" under Khrushchev Boky was "rehabilitated" and his good reputation restored posthumously in June of 1956.

## Mass Murder as the Secret of Social Revolution

Anyone who has read about the Imperial Russian efforts to suppress the revolutionaries of the day will be impressed with the relative leniency with which they treated the insurgents. They would be exiled for a while, put in some distant village for a few years, some were killed in street demonstrations or in prisons or actually executed, but relatively few. Certainly, the Bolsheviks learned by this "bad" example. The Tsar had signed his own death-warrant with his leniency. They would not make such a mistake. In an effort to revolutionize society in the most radical ways, the population *could* (theoretically) be educated or re-educated to accept Marxist-Leninist principles, or, alternatively, the undesirable or deplorable elements or difficult populations (Ukrainians, Cossacks, etc.) could just be decimated or eliminated, thus freeing the state from the onerous and difficult task of arguing its case with stubborn groups. This may not have been the original plan behind the Red Terror (August-November, 1918), but its benefits were soon learned and the technique implemented repeatedly throughout the Stalinist years in the use of famine in Ukraine (1932-1933) or the Great Purge of 1937-1938. The history of this has been substantially covered by R. J. Rummel (2017). The original Red Terror was well-noted by Hitler and used as a model for "cultural reform" in National Socialist Germany. The Marxist-Leninist formula was generally said to call for the elimination of approximately ten percent of the population, those most likely to resist the "reforms" being implemented by the new regime. Ironically, of course, actual membership in the ruling Communist Party in the post-Revolutionary societies was also generally set to constitute no more than around ten percent of the general population. In a manner of speaking we are dealing with a sort of "philosophical cleansing."

This method became a textbook strategy in most countries in which Marxist-Leninist Revolution was tried. Just to name a few of the most significant examples, we have China — the Land Reform, Counter-Revolutionary Eliminations, Great Leap Forward and the Cultural Revolution were all reiterations of this program. Similar programs were carried out in Tibet and other minority areas within the Red Chinese / Han empire. Beyond these examples, and as a demonstration that this pattern in fact became a standard part of Marxist-Leninist strategy, we also have Ethiopia with its own Red Terror (1977-1978) and the famous example of Cambodia and its infamous Killing Fields. The millions upon millions that have fallen victim to Red Terrors in one place or another obviously dwarf the National Socialist-engineered Holocaust in Germany as regards raw numbers, but it is a curious fact that no one has ever been held accountable criminally for any of this activity by the so-called Left. There must be some sort of sorcery in that as well.

## Bolshevik Symbolism

As we have seen, the Silver Age in Russia, the time in which Lenin came of political and philosophical age, was extremely rich in symbolic and occult ideas. These ideas gave a new, more *Russian* shape to Marxist theory. For the Symbolist the *word*, the poetic expression of ideas in verbal form, had the power to embody reality and the poet seized the power to wield the meaning of words to alter the shape of the future. This ideology is extended to all forms of symbolism— graphic, architectural, cinematic, etc.

Irina Gutkin in her article "The Magic of Words" (1997.pp. 239-40) says:

> The Bolshevik coup put an end to the search for such a design by installing Marxism as the comprehensive doctrine that connected all the phenomena of the universe, thus fulfilling in a new way the aspirations of occult philosophers. Most important, Marxism claimed to be the ultimate expression of the "objective laws of history." All that was left for scientists and philosophers was to supplement "the only true scientific teaching" as Marxism cum Leninism cum Stalinism and beyond came to be called — by extending its reach to all spheres of knowledge about life and the universe. ... Needless to say, the official formula underscores the all-pervading hegemony of Marxism , under which there could be no place for any rival system, particularly a religious or occult one. The mysticism of predictive magic was supplanted by the mystique of science. In the rhetorical climate where any notion deemed politically incorrect was derisively condemned as "pseudo-scientific," all manner of occult beliefs and magic practices were severely ostracized as "unscientific" and therefore harmful.

Lenin's Tomb in Red Square in Moscow

As most people are aware, the body of V. I. Lenin was elaborately preserved and is to this day still on display within his tomb on Red Square. The reasons for this public display of his undecayed remains are complex and multilayered. The main two reasons speak to two extremes in Russian society: to the peasantry and residual Orthodox believers and their folklore and more importantly to the visionary Bolsheviks themselves and to the Cosmist element among them. In ancient Russian (and Slavic) folklore the fate of the body of a dead person could go one of three different ways: a normal person simply rots away, leaving only bones, a vampire remains intact, but turns bluish-black and is swollen with the blood of its victims, but a saint will remain as he was in life, sweet smelling and pink. For the peasant mindset Lenin is on display as a saint. But, as we have seen with the Cosmist theories of Fedorov and others, it was considered a possibility that one day the dead would be resurrected by means of science and that they would additionally be rendered immortal. Lenin's body is kept in a state of suspended existence artificially (scientifically) awaiting the moment when this technology is perfected and he can return and govern his machine in his infinite wisdom. For a time, Stalin's body was similarly prepared and Joe rested beside Lenin with his name receiving second billing on the façade of the tomb. (Stalin's body was removed from the tomb in 1961, and he was reburied in a place of honor along the Kremlin wall.

## The Symbols of Bolshevism

The hammer and sickle stands for worker-peasant alliance: the hammer is a traditional symbol of proletariat and the sickle is a traditional symbol for the peasantry. The symbol evolved over a few years' time. The basic idea of combining symbols of industry and agriculture, the workers and the peasants, was the common theme of several designs— a hammer and sickle, a hammer and rakes, a hammer and pitchforks, and a hammer and plow… The final design created by the artist Yevgeny Kamzolkin was accepted by the party in April of 1918 and became official in the summer of that year. Oddly, Kamzolkin was not a Communist at all and was a member of a mystical artistic group called the Society of Leonardo da Vinci. The pagan thunder-god, Svarog, wielded a hammer as a weapon against the forces of evil, while the goddess Mara or Morana traditionally held a sickle in her left hand. Whatever its other connotations the symbol is one of the unity of the workers and farmers of the world.

Another symbol of Communism in Russia is the five-pointed solid red star. A version of it also appeared on the flag of the USSR. The most exoteric meaning of it is that it is a symbol of the Red Army, of the military wing of the state. There are several explanations of its deeper meaning, but it should be noted that on an esoteric level the five-pointed star can be taken as a sign of Mars (the Red Planet) and of Man. In the real context of contemporaneous Russian culture of the day, however, many believe that the best explanation of it and its allure for the people is its origin in the popular science fiction novel *Red Star* (1908) by Alexander Bogdanov. It is set in the time of the 1905 Revolution and in a socialist society based on the planet Mars. The story tells of a Russian scientist and revolutionary named Leonid who travels to Mars to learn about and experience the socialist system of the Martians so that he can teach about its wondrous technology and efficiency to his comrades in Russia.

Another interesting character in this world was one Alexander Agienko who took the name of an ancient pagan Russian mythical demigod (*bogatyr*) named Svyatogor. Agienko was a "performance artist" of sorts, who performed publicity stunts for his cause of being a "biochemist." He also called himself the "Rooster of Revolution." His wild and eccentric speeches consistently called for the achievement of immortality, the resurrection of the dead and the colonization of outer space. (Young 2012: 197-199)

Clearly, one of the great things that separates Cosmist Bolshevism from ordinary Bolshevism is the degree to which the former is based on an optimistic and positive outlook, whereas the latter is bent only on the acquisition, exercise and maintenance of materialistic political power. The former desires only what is best and most optimal for all humans, whereas the latter is motivated as much by the hatred of some "other" group as it is by a lust for power pertaining to the Party. It has often been wondered how the Bolsheviks maintained power while performing so badly in economic terms for the workers and peasants. The answer was often, sadly, that the Communist Revolutionary could be miserable, but was satisfied if those he was taught to hate were made to be more miserable than he.

# 4. The Age of Stalin

A Genuine Photograph of Joseph Stalin

Stalin (meaning "steely") was the cover-name for Ioseb Besarionis dze Djugashvili (1878-1953), an ethnic Georgian. His full Russified names was Joseph Vissarionovich Stalin. After the Revolution, he legally changed his name to the Russified form. His family was poor and he joined the RSDLP while still very young. He was clever, and even studied at a seminary for a while. He edited the Party's newspaper *Pravda* ("Truth") for a whole. But Stalin was also at heart a thug. He raised funds for Lenin's Party with typical gangster schemes: protection rackets, robberies and kidnappings. When the Bolsheviks seized power, Stalin served on the Politburo from the beginning. He fought in the Civil War and was a guiding force in the establishment of the Soviet Union. He became the General Secretary of the Communist Party in 1922 and remained in that post for most of the rest of his life. He also became Premier of the Soviet Union in 1941— and made the famous non-aggression pact with Hitler. After Lenin's death in 1924 Stalin governed as part of a collective leadership, but by the mid-1930s he had become the strongman dictator of the USSR. He took every opportunity to consolidate his power, usually at the expense of men who had talent and ability, and who he in some way saw as a threat. He cracked down on the whole Cosmist trend and anything that has a whiff of the avant-garde. His draconian Five Year Plans led to worsening economic conditions and even famines (also intentionally used as genocidal weapon in Ukraine, for example). The Great Purge went on from 1934 to 1939. The reader will note how often, when discussing many of the interesting thinkers in this book, they ended their lives being annihilated by the Stalinist Purge. All vision and imagination was pressed out of the system in favor of the crushing weight of "historical materialist" orthodoxy. Stalin managed the military victory of the Red Army over the Nazis in 1945, and then engineered, with the help of the Western Allies, the virtual annexation of all of eastern Europe as puppet states of the Soviet Union. He also oversaw the spread of Communism to the East in China and North Korea. Politically and ideologically Stalin departed from the principles of Leninism and established what must be called Stalinism. In propaganda and historical representations, his personality came to supersede even that of Lenin. After WWII Stalin continued in his old habits of mismanagement and use of famines as weapons against his own people. Stalin engaged in Anti-Semitic campaigns and show trials as control mechanisms.

Despite the fact that Stalin was hostile (officially) to ideas of Cosmism and the like, he apparently did practice his own form of magic, as we will see. But this was reserved to him alone.

After his death, it fell to Nikita Khrushchev to denounce Stalin as a dictator and to undertake the de-Stalinization of the USSR. As I have said, Stalin's body was originally placed in Lenin's Tomb alongside the first leader of the Bolsheviks. Today Stalin enjoys a renewed popularity among some Russians, but besides his role in WWII he has little to recommend him in the history of the Russian people. His systematic dismantling of the creative Cosmist spirit of the Party of Lenin ensured the ultimate demise of the USSR and the ultimate failure of the Soviet system. The cultural damage he did was just far too great.

Although we do not much associate Stalin with occult thinking, not to do so would be wrong. Stalin was hard-headed, pragmatic, violent, paranoid (with good reason) and apparently highly superstitious. It is also not unthinkable that he was steeped in occult thinking.

It appears to be a certain fact that Stalin knew G. I. Gurdjieff. When Djugashvili was a seminary student in Tiflis he rented a room with the Gurdjieff family. It is there that it is said Joseph and George became friends and that at one point Joseph accompanied Gurdjieff on one of his trips to the East. It is likely that in all of this Djugashvili was involved in some sort of intelligence work, which he might have done for Tsarist interests in exchange for release from prison. Gurdjieff too was probably in some way involved in the Great Game.

It is well-known that Stalin bore the nick-name "Koba." This was supposed to mean something like "sorcerer" or "prophet," and which is also supposedly connected with a Persian ruler named Kobadesa from the 5$^{th}$ century. This must be a garbled reference to the Sassanian Emperor Kavâd I, who reigned between 488 and 496 then again from 498 to 531. At that time, Georgia was part of the Persian Empire. Kavâd is transliterated into Greek as Kabates and into Arabic as Qubâdh. It is further stated that this emperor was involved in an ideology which had some similarities to Communism. In fact, this Kavâd I did have an ambivalent link with the doctrines of Mazdak, a Zoroastrian reformer who taught a sort of ancient Communism. (See the Appendix to this book: Esoteric Bolshevism and Zoroastrian Tradition.)

When Lenin died in 1924 Joseph Stalin began to consolidate his power from his position as General Secretary of the Communist Party. In 1929 Stalin's chief rival for power, Leon Trotsky, was exiled to Mexico and Stalin's hold on ideological power was complete. Stalin reinstated a regime of cultural conservatism and virtually every shred of the *avant-garde* characteristics of the Revolution under Lenin was suppressed. To his citizens, Stalin became a devil incarnate perhaps liquidating as many of his countrymen as were killed by the Germans in the "Great Patriotic War" (as WWII is called by the Russians. Any and all popular deviations from the strict, atheistically puritanical code of Stalinist authoritarianism became impossible except deep within cells of the secret state apparatus, which were also subject to arbitrary periodic purges and terror campaigns.

Stalin wielded the idea of orthodox Marxism-Leninism as a club with which he could smash any enemy ideologically before he actually annihilated them both physically and even erased their memories from history. The theoretically Marxist-Leninist line of thought was utterly (if covertly or *secretly*) rejected by Stalin during his tenure as Soviet dictator. For all intents and purposes the Marxist-Leninist experiment died in the Stalinist purges. What replaced it was the ever-popular form of simple tyranny, with symbolic and formal flourishes and the occasional theoretical outcropping of actual Leninist theory. Part of Stalin's sorcery was to eradicate the image of Lenin and replace it with his own. This went so far as the re-editing of propaganda films first to bolster the role of Stalin in the 1917 Revolution and then to make Lenin disappear from the scenes entirely! (Imagine what a Stalin could do with the Internet.)

# Stalin and Language

As Stalin began his rule, Soviet linguistics was dominated by the ideas of Nikolai Yakovievich Marr who held that language itself is a "class construction" and that its conventions and structures are determined by economic configurations and rules. This jargon, rooted in esoteric dimensions of historical materialism, is once more heard in the West among academics, who claim that biological realities such as "gender" or "race" are actually "social" or "linguistic constructs." Stalin, who had an interest in languages himself, took exception to the Marxist formalism displayed by Marr's theories and undertook to oppose them in an essay entitled "Marxism and Linguistic Questions" (1950).

The linguistic dimension of the practice of Red Magic, or socialist linguistic operations, were best and most vividly explained and demonstrated in the fictional and philosophical works of George Orwell, e.g. "Politics and the English Language" (1946), *Animal Farm* (1945) and *Nineteen Eighty-Four* (1948). His explanation of Newspeak by which words are given meanings by political authorities and enforced into the popular language through the media has today become a reality.

Stalin's foray into the world of linguistics was studied by Pawel Nowak and Rafal Zimny in an article entitled "Joseph Stalin's statements on language and linguistics as verbal acts of autocracy" which gives insight into the motives behind his interest:

> Stalin's final aim was to declare his power over language. He knew that language is the key to human spirituality, for it links thinking of, experiencing and understanding the world. Therefore, he proposed a conception of language as a tool, added a political dimension to knowledge about language and assigned to linguists the role of investigators of the laws of development of language structure. His aim was to render difficult or even completely thwart reflection on semantic and communicative processes because such reflection could reveal changes in the Russian language after the October Revolution. It could also disturb the monolith of the nation ruled by an autocratic despot. Aleksander Wat describes this situation as follows:
>
>> Stalinism consists in a systematic instrumentalization of everything: the world of humans and the world of things. All human economic, social and spiritual activity; an instrumentalization of people themselves, their consciousness, thoughts and words, and finally of the doctrine itself.
>
> (Nowak and Zimny 2014, p. 73)

During the Stalinist Era, the magical use of language in settings of political ritualism reached a high-point, as described here:

> The standard practice of relentlessly chanting the Supreme Leader's name or such slogans as "Lenin lived, Lenin lives, Lenin will live!" at Party congresses and public forums suggests invocation of deities or the casting of a magic spell. Even if the initiators and enthusiastic mass perpetrators of this custom had no such conscious intent, these rituals worked to hypnotize participating audiences into a state of ecstatic frenzy. The stenographic reports of the grandiose state and Party congresses of the Stalin era record in formulaic phrases how the "storms of applause" that punctuated the speeches of the Supreme Ideologue escalated into protracted "standing ovations" (a practice that, together with other such ritualistic pomp, persisted into the post-Stalin era, if on a reduced scale.
>
> (Gutkin, 1997: 243)

## Science in the Age of Stalin

During the Stalinist Era a number of unusual, some might say, occult, scientific projects were undertaken. However, the time period is most marked by the suppression of various sorts of study, or their ideological direction under the influence of historical materialism dictated by Marxist-Leninist theory as Stalin often capriciously interpreted this idea. Both the humanities and hard sciences were subjected to ideological litmus tests. Of course, just as the Christian Middle Ages which subjected thinkers to ideological tests, such an approach will severely handicap the free pursuit of science.

Soviet science, as well as its politics, followed Marxist-Leninist methods of having an *ideological* model guide the thinking of those who come to a consensus on any question, then that conclusion is determined (in accordance with ideology) and subsequently the whole of the body politic is required to hold the same conclusion, then implement and adopt that conclusion as their own. Consensus = Reality: There is great sorcery in that formulation.

All of Soviet scientific scholarship read like some sort of homily. Whatever the study, it had to be predicated by, and have frequent quotes from, what were considered Marxist-Leninist philosophical "classics." In the 1930s the archives of the state and party were generally closed to scholars, so the past was what contemporary ideology allowed it to be. Pre-Revolutionary history, especially Russian history, had to be subjected to ideological criticism in light of the current Party Line. A cynic would simply see this as the exercise of power and control, and that was probably true then, as it is now when people try to do similar things. But within the rationale of the ideology, it was a sort of mythologizing of the past in accordance with the ideals of the present moment in order to build the future envisioned in Marxism-Leninism. The world was being remade, and an effective tool for this was the remaking of the past to accord with the more perfect future.

Ideological correctness was reality, if then a dissident disagreed with a point of ideology, he or she was not merely a rebel or a political nonconformist, rather he or she was actually mentally ill, insane— out of touch with reality. This is how mental institutions became political prisons and re-education centers in the Soviet Union.

The study of genetics in the Soviet Union was greatly compromised by ideological criticisms. The science was on the one hand criticized due to the fact that the Nazis extoled it, and on the other hand because its direction, as practiced in the West, tended toward what the Stalinists would call "idealism," and so it violated strict and simple historical materialist notions. The very fact that the founder of the science of genetics, Gregor Mendel, had been a Catholic monk made it problematic for Soviet ideologues. Soviet biology fell under the dogma of what was called the Pavlovian session. Any "hard science" was a political problem for Stalinist ideologues simply because the results were difficult to manipulate in favor of those in power. *Everything* was to be open to modification based on ideology.

Under Stalin, Soviet sciences of biology and agronomy fell under the pseudo-scientist Trofim Denisovich Lysenko (1898-1976). He wrote an article in *Pravda* about his ideas connecting the growth of plants with Lamarckian ideas. This came to the attention of Stalin and thus Lysenko became a prominent theorist for the Party in biology. Stalin and other ideologues approved of him for his strong anti-Mendelian stance. Lysenko came from peasant stock and was largely "self-taught." He came to argue against the Darwinian concept of competition among species, and claimed that even plants could exercise "mutual assistance" not only within species, but between species as well. Lysenko carved out a powerful niche for himself in the hierarchy of the Party, and he himself practiced the sort of competition he denied to the plants. Those who opposed him and his theories were denounced as "unscientific." He had the full support of Stalin in his endeavors. He became director of the Institute of Genetics in 1940 and his influence became even more draconian. He asserted things such as "mathematics has no place in biology." Those scientists who refused to renounce "the monk," Mendel, were dismissed from their posts and left without support, thousands of others were even imprisoned or put in mental "hospitals" and some were executed as enemies of the state. Disagreement with Lysenko or his theory of environmentally acquired inheritance was actually criminalized in 1948. The problem was that his ideas were entirely pseudoscientific fantasies and what is more they did not work. But because he was supported by Stalin they were promoted and implemented. Great and permanent harm was done to Soviet science and economy, people died of famine, but any and all failures of Lysenko's ideas were routinely blamed on "bourgeois saboteurs" and "tools of imperialist oppressors." The fact that Lysenko had no qualifications to do the work he was supposedly carrying out recommended him highly in the eyes of Stalinist ideology, dedicated to promoting members of the proletariat to positions of power. After Stalin's death, Lysenko's power was greatly diminished, but he hung on for years to come, keeping Soviet science in a backward state until he was finally dismissed in 1965 and disgraced through exposés of his methods and theories.

Men such as Lysenko and those who promoted them, such as Stalin, doomed the Soviet Union to its ultimate fate. It was state-suicide by ideology. This was slowly realized by a minority of thinking and imaginative Soviet citizens from the 1960s forward— but it was far too late. When the "great" Lysenko died in 1976 his death received only a small note in *Izvestia*.

"Cybernetics" a book and concept put forward by Norbert Wiener in 1948, which was the beginning of modern computer technology in the West, was roundly condemned by Stalin as a bourgeois pseudoscience and somehow contrary to the "materialistic dialectics" of Ivan Pavlov. Stalinists were addicted to referring to Pavlov when condemning scientists they did not like. Usually this had nothing to do with what Pavlov actually thought or taught. This Soviet rejection of the concept set back computer technology in the USSR a decade or more at a time when this was crucial to their position in relation to the USA in the Cold War. Again, the rejection of forward-looking visionary thought in favor of ham-fisted ideology eventually sealed the fate of the Soviet Union. Repeatedly throughout the history of the USSR we see that hard science was subjected to ideological or political criteria and this attitude acted as a malignancy in the system that eventually helped bring about its downfall.

History itself held a special place in Soviet science, of course. History as a topic was something that was under the strict control and direction of Soviet authorities with the aim of furthering the cause and purpose of the

Revolution and consolidating and expanding Soviet power globally. There was a Party Line on most questions, including history, and this was ideologically identified as being something that was concurrent with reality or truth.

Despite the theoretical and doctrinal attitude of the Soviets toward internationalism and the theoretical distaste for "nationalism" as such, there remained in the Russian-dominated Soviet system a strong thread of Pan-Slavic nationalism. This would rear its head in historical discussions, for example around that question of the origins of the Russian state. The well-known and established role of the Scandinavian Rûs (Varangians, Swedish "Vikings") in establishing early kingdoms in Slavic territories were generally denied and events such as those described by Ibn Fadlan in his famous account were ascribed to Slavs rather than Scandinavians for reasons of nationalistic pride. Of course, in reality these were not questions of the struggles of nation-states at all, but rather groups of individual men belonging to warrior-bands, trade associations (guilds) who just happened to be Swedes. In any event, it is true that the Scandinavians in question were fairly quickly "Slaviciszed" linguistically.

In more recent years, Russian nationalists have turned more to their Nordic, Viking, roots in a search for a more effective mythic identity, and so the Soviet-inspired Slavophilic rift in history can be seen to have been greatly healed.

In the area of physics, the doctrine of dialectical materialism proved to be a great hindrance to the development of up-to-date research in vital fields of aerospace and nuclear physics. Theories such as quantum mechanics, general and special relativity were all criticized by ideologues on the basis that they were too "idealistic." No politically correct physics was ever posited or proven, and so ways had to be found around this particular conundrum in order for Soviet science to have any hope of keeping up with the West. This story is reminiscent of the way in which National Socialists criticized Einstein's theories as being "Jewish physics," and tried to develop an "Aryan physics" using the theories of men such as Hanns Hörbiger.

# Vladimir Vernadsky

## Vladimir Ivanovich Vernadsky

Vladimir Ivanovich Vernadsky (1863-1945) was a geochemist and mineralogist who pioneered such sciences as biogeochemistry and radiogeology. He is best known for his 1926 book *The Biosphere*, which popularized the term coined originally by the Austrian Eduard Suess in 1885, whom Vernadsky met in 1911. Vernadsky theorized that life itself is a geological force that participates in shaping and reshaping the planet. He received the Stalin Prize in 1943. He studied in Munich and Jena in the 1880s where he investigated the crystallization process. Before he resigned from his post in protest in 1911, he was a professor at Moscow University.

In Russia, he was political from an early time and in connection with the 1905 revolution he participated in meetings on how to pressure the Tsar into making reforms. At first, he was a member of the Constitutional Democratic Party. He took various posts in the government after the Revolution in 1917.

Vernadsky was the first to bring the concept of the noosphere to the attention of the public, and broadened awareness of the idea of the biosphere, one that has become a generally accepted concept among many scientists of today.

Vernadsky introduced an evolutionary theory concerning the earth's development in which there is envisioned a transition from the original geosphere (inanimate matter), to the biosphere (living matter), with a coming phase called the noosphere (realm of reason). Vernadsky's theories took these ideas into a more developmental realm. The noosphere is seen as the third level of the evolution of the planet. So, below it remains the biosphere encompassing biological life forms, and below that is the geosphere comprising all inanimate matter also continues to exist. Each level on the planet evolved after the previous one, and as the next level evolves, it at the same time fundamentally transforms the level that lies beneath it and upon which it is founded. As the development of life-forms changed the nature of the inanimate portions of the planet, so too will the evolution of consciousness profoundly alter and develop "lower" life forms. Vernadsky maintained that the structures of life and consciousness were latent in the composition of the planet from the beginning, but that as they develop or evolve they gain greater dominance and impact.

In many ways Vernadsky's theories completed and contextualized Darwin's theories of evolution in that Vernadsky systemically examined the environmental interconnection between the various species and their "subsuming principles." He was also among the first scientists to realize that the oxygen, nitrogen and carbon dioxide in the Earth's atmosphere are actually the byproducts of biological processes. Furthermore, he wrote that living organisms have the capacity to shape and reshape the environments of planets. These concepts act as an introduction to the concept of terraforming planets making them fit for habitation by colonizing Earthlings. On a cultural level Vernadsky was a supporter of the idea of Eurasianism which continues to exert a powerful force in Russian politics today.

Although Vernadsky maintained that he was an orthodox Marxist and atheist he is also known to have had a great interest in the ideas contained in Hinduism and especially those of the *Rig Veda*.

## The Continuation of Russian Mysticism

It is worth pointing out that when Fulop-Miller published *The Mind and Face of Bolshevism* in 1927 he included a whole chapter (pages 255-264) on the persistence of the mystical dimensions of Russian Orthodoxy. Despite all efforts by the Soviet government to eradicate religion from the lives of the people these old religions patterns, with some of their roots going back to pre-Christian times in Russia, continued to make their influences felt. It appears at Russian mysticism endured as a secret tradition even within the membership of the Communist Party. This also goes a long way toward explaining its vibrant renewal in post-Soviet Russia.

# Alexander Chizhevsky

Alexander Chizhevsky Explaining his Theories

On a much more scientific note we have Alexander Leonidovich Chizhevsky (1897-1964), an unconventional thinker who developed several theories and practices which might be considered occult by some. He called himself a biophysicist and founded the study of heliobiology, or the effect of the sun and its phenomena (e.g. sun-spots) on biological entities on Earth. He also explored the effects of "aero-ionization," that is the ionization of the air and its influence on living organisms. Politically, Chizhevsky was able to survive the Stalin years without being liquidated, but did spend some years in a Gulag for having questionable theories. Chizhevsky's father, although an ethnic Pole, was a general in the Russian army. Chizhevsky spent his younger years in the town of Kaluga, where he met Konstantin Tsiolkovsky. Even in his youth he was observing solar activity and its effects on human behavior. While serving in the Russian army during WWI he observed that battles became more or less intense based on solar flare activity. Chizhevsky completed his studies at the Moscow Commercial Institute in archeology with a doctoral dissertation entitled "On the periodicity of the world-historical process." His theories of cyclical patterns in history based on solar activity would later be termed heliotaraxy or heliotaraxia. He also continued his studies with ionization, and established that negatively charged ions led to a high level of stimulation in living organisms, while positively charged ones led to lethargy.

In 1926, Chizhevsky again crossed paths with Konstantin Tsiolkovsky and he collaborated with him in experimental work in the area of space biology. The next year he entered the Tulan Academy and even lectured at Columbia University in New York.

It would seem that Chizhevsky's work remained well within the materialistic model demanded by Marxist orthodoxy, however, when Stalin learned of his work, especially one entitled *Physical Factors of the Historical Process* (1926), it was requested that the scientist retract and denounce his theory since his ideas seemed to run counter to the current official explanations and understandings of the causes of the Revolutions of 1905 and 1917. When he refused to recant, he was sentenced to eight years of forced labor in the Ural Mountains. When he was "released" he was conveniently resettled in Karaganda in Kazakhstan where he enjoyed eight more years of "rehabilitation" during which time he did scientific work down in the coal mines. After that he lost interest in writing about the solar cycle theory. I guess the re-education worked.

When he returned to Moscow he introduced the idea of aero-ionic therapy (negative air ionization therapy). These theories were better received by the Party and he was able to continue with this work in medical facilities and in state offices. He lived and worked in Kaluga for a period and reconnected with Tsiolkovsky.

It was Chizhevsky's theory that geomagnetic storms connected to sunspot activity influence electrical usage, plane crashes, epidemics and grasshopper infestations, as well as human mental health and level of activity. He determined that increased negative ionization of the atmosphere leads to an elevation in mass human mental stimulation and can lead to mass movements of people in history to engage in revolts, revolutions and conflicts or wars in general. He further claimed that these events occurred in cycles of eleven years.

Despite the fact that his theories hardly seem to accord with Western ideas of science, and despite the fact that Stalin saw fit to "re-educate" him, Chizhevsky's ideas continue to excite some attention and respect. Chizhevsky has come to be recognized as one who discovered the energetic relationship between the Sun and living organisms on Earth. In the 1960s the Soviet Academy of Sciences re-examined Chizhevsky's archived research and it was determined that his findings were legitimate and some said worthy of the Nobel Prize, if he had only not been branded a "heretic" and sent to a gulag! In more recent years Chizhevsky's ideas both in regard to solar activity and ionization of the air have gained wider interest and even acceptance.

It is noteworthy that Chizhevsky was also a painter of water colors which were shown in Soviet galleries and was also the author of hundreds of poems. He was another of those rare truly Renaissance Men of the Revolution.

## Stalinist Occultism

As might be expected, overt occult ideas and publications were strictly forbidden in the Stalinist era. There was an insistence on the concept that the state and Stalin himself were exponents of science and the rational. But in fact, the use of occult techniques was rampant in this time period. So-called Socialist Realism in art and literature is full of occult meaning. The whole propagandistic thrust of the state was the idea of the "conquest of nature." Stalin and the state were focused on creating miracles, or at least making people believe that miracles were possible and taking place all around. Optimism in literature and film was used in a consciously hypnotic manner. It was believed that Stalin could change the climate with his mere presence. When Five Year Plans failed, these failures were always blamed on "wreckers and saboteurs" who were the functional equivalent of black magicians or witches in the folk-belief of ancient Russia. Even the show trials of Stalin's enemies (real and imagined) had the occult dimension that it was believed that logical or rational evidence brought on behalf of the defense was useless because the state authorities held that "empirical reality does not exist." (Rosenthal, p. 17) In Stalinism nature becomes subject to ideological reconstruction.

One writer, Lev Kopelev (1980, p. 262), notes that Stalin's interminable speeches had the quality of incantations with an emphasis on monotony and what he called "mumbo-jumbo" which is compared to the utterances of shamans. Stalin was obsessed with the power of words and so only an approved formulaic vocabulary was sanctioned and other elements strictly censored.

Finally, it might be noted that the very name of Stalin was invested with magical powers by fighters in the Great Patriotic War (= WWII) when his name was called upon for protection and as they went into battle they called out "For the homeland! For Stalin!"


## Stalin's Witch

Although almost nothing is known about her, Natalia Lvova is said to have been Stalin's secret advisor on matters of the occult and "supernatural." She was apparently a practitioner of Russian folk-magic and healing methods. The only known photograph of her shows her in a nurse's uniform, probably from the time of the First World War. She advised Uncle Joe on matters that were entirely personal to him, but which greatly affected politics and world affairs. She advised him not to allow himself to be photographed. It is thought that most of the photos of Stalin are actually of his double. The one at the head of section 5.1 is said to be genuine as he has his eyes closed. Natalia's assignment was to protect the Supreme Leader from the effects of the "evil eye," or any magical means arrayed against him from his opponents. She advised him on matters of who to allow into his inner circle, and who needed to be removed.  She was a third-generation "witch," and the daughter of a St. Petersburg clairvoyant. Stalin summoned her to Moscow in 1930.

Natalia Lvova

Lvova's activities and details about her must have assumed the highest level of secrecy, as even today little more is known of her.

# 5. Post-Stalinist Ages
## Soviet Period after Stalin

When Stalin died, he left the Soviet Union in a terrible state. It had for almost thirty years become totally dependent upon his personality, his tyranny and brutality— the *numinosum tremendum* — the terrifying presence — had departed, leaving his world without meaning. The Revolution of Lenin and the other "Old Bolsheviks" had long since faded into vague memory. Those left behind really did not know what to do, but they did muddle on for almost forty more years! The Revolution of 1917 promised a vision of the future, Stalin had robbed it of that, and it proved impossible to regain the old vision collectively or to generate a new one.

Nevertheless, there were several great achievements of the Soviet Union in the post-Stalinist era, but they little helped the masses in their quest for a better life. There was the launch of Sputnik in 1957 and the space flight of Yuri Gagarin in 1961. But still the grain harvest was unreliable and often the shoe-store had only left-footed shoes to sell...

One Cosmist thinker who survived into the post-Stalinist Age was Vasily Kuprevich (1897-1969). He was able to steer clear of ideological controversy, while still doing ground-breaking research and suggesting radical ideas. He was also a Deputy of the Supreme Soviet (1952-1969), but we have seen that high political placement is not necessarily a guarantee against persecution. But Kuprevich did become active only in the post-Stalinist period which made a huge difference in men's fates. His main area of Cosmist research was in the field of immortality studies. He followed Fedorov and stated that death was an acquired characteristic of the species and could be equated with some sort of genetic disorder. The area he is best known for researching is that of botany, where he studied the possibility of immortality based on the characteristics found in certain plants which enjoy extreme longevity.

## Revival of God-Building

Nine years after Stalin's death Soviet officials began to rethink the methods and policies Stalin had pursued against religious practices. The All-Union Conference on Scientific Propaganda discussed the concept of educating the populace in not only Communist ethics and philosophy, but also institute customs, rituals and traditions to replace traditional religious forms. It seems that after four decades of attempting to eradicate religion and the religious feeling in the Russian populace, at least some were beginning to see the wisdom of men such as Lunacharsky and Bonch-

Bruyevich who had wanted to engage in the project of God-Building and make use of the human desire for ritual and custom. Of course, it would eventually be shown that the damage done in those four decades was irreparable.

In the mid-1960s Khrushchev renewed critical attacks on religion, but they seemed to have no effect in the popular mind. Certain ideologues began to publish ideas that once more brought back Lunacharsky's concepts surrounding God-Building. Rituals were suggested which would forge a mystical link between the people and the promised Communist society which would have its dawn in the future. It was suggested that temples exemplifying the glories of a future Communism, thought to be man's greatest possible achievement, should be built. There it was envisioned that orations would be performed to instruct the masses in Communist doctrines. It is certain that the time for such efforts had long faded into history— but it was the '60s— even in Soviet Russia!

However, the new "God-Builders" were not as radical or far-sighted as Lunacharsky had been. They carefully attempted to find ways around Lenin's earlier criticism of the idea. Few practical goals were realized, but some new rituals were developed for certain official events, e.g. in 1966 there was an "All-Union Day of the Agricultural Worker" which took structural elements from traditional rituals connected with St. John the Baptist's Day.

In the Ukraine, there was instituted celebration called the Holiday of the Hammer and Sickle. It has been described as follows:

> On an early December morning tractor drivers |from the surrounding region| converge in <u>Zhytomyr</u>. At the entry to the city they are met by the representatives of the city factories who report to them on the progress of the socialist emulation and invite the drivers to their factories, where the peasants and the workers engage in heart-searching and business like discussions. Then a parade of agrarian technology takes place at the Lenin Square. Solemnly, accompanied by an orchestra, the best workers and peasants receive their prizes and diplomas. Then all of them make public production-quota pledges for the forthcoming year at the city theatre.
>
> (Pospielovsky 1987: 96)

In the 1960s there began to be instituted certain rites and ceremonies such as one for receiving a passport on one's sixteenth birthday, or for an initiation into the ranks of the workers or peasants. In the late 1950s, secular ceremonies were devised for civil marriages, name-giving rites for babies and funerals.

It seems that in certain geographical regions the church had been eliminated altogether. In these places, it seems that paganism, that is indigenous native religion, started to remanifest itself. The idea of God-Building tended to make strong inroads into these very communities.

Although the Soviet authorities would often claim that they were making progress toward eliminating the church from people's lives, after seventy years of Socialism the fact that the Russian Orthodox Church made such a comeback in public life after its official demise during the Soviet period demonstrates that these claims were false. Orthodox rites and customs were simply carried out in secret.

Of course, all of these efforts were far too little and far too late to save the Soviet Union. The USSR did not collapse because it failed to institute various sorts of rites and rituals, but rather because it failed to synthesize the most radical elements of Russian Cosmism into its ideology which might have helped it keep up with Western innovations.

## The Age of Putin

The rapid and complete abandonment of official Communist ideological orthodoxy by the ruling elite in Russia beginning in 1991 is a clear historical demonstration of one overriding point: The rulers did not actually "believe" the theory, it was merely a means to an end: the acquisition and maintenance of power for the ruling elite itself. As soon as the system did not work anymore, and as soon as certain individuals were in a position to make use of a better mode of attaining the all-important goal, the old theory was dropped. Marxist-Leninist orthodoxy had lost its theoretical advantage and had become a burden and hindrance to the desired ends. The fact that the old Communists never lost control of the state is one of the most important facts about the new Russia. It was just that the "old racket" didn't work as well as a new racket promised to do. The new Russian government retains all of the old apparatus of the Bolshevik state with new names, but the whole operates on a much more flexible and pragmatic basis. The Left in the West, still sentimentally believing in the theoretical foundations of Bolshevism has turned on Russia. The old Bolsheviks were far more self-aware and conscious of what they were doing than the "cultural Marxists" of the West are today. To the Russian, Marxism was a "cover story" for a criminal racket, in the West it has become for some a new religion with real "true believers." But the aims for both are equally the same: the acquisition and maintenance of personal power for members of the ruling elite in the guise of a "good cause."

As I have noted, it appears that the Bolsheviks were mainly a gang of operators who pulled the biggest of all possible heists. They high-jacked a whole country, as poor as it was, and confiscated for their personal use the entire means of production possessed by anyone in that state.

The current American political establishment does not know what to make of Russia or its leader, Vladimir Putin. Political discourse in the USA seems of late to have descended to the level of argumentation one might remember from one's elementary school days. When kids argue among themselves, the only semblance of principle that arises in such debates is that "Joey said it, I hate Joey, so the statement is false," or Joey's on the B-team, I'm on the A-team, Joey's wrong, Joey's a liar." In the 1960s, during the Vietnam War, liberals would constantly say things such as: "The Soviets aren't so bad. They have their hearts in the right place. Besides, America is just as bad. Why can't we just get along?" These attitudes were instilled by the propaganda machine of the Soviet Union and struck deep roots. Current liberals came of age during the time of the anti-Vietnam War protest movement. This movement is now considered to have been a breeding ground of "higher political virtues." As this book has shown, the skill and experience of the Bolsheviks in crafting operative communications are considerable, and have roots that go back to the Tsarist times. In his memoires, colonel Stanislav Lunev of the GRU stated that the Soviet his agency spent more money funding the anti-Vietnam War movement in the US than they did arming the Viet-Cong. Propaganda proved a more effective weapon than bombs. Anyone who tried to point out Soviet manipulation of domestic protest culture at that time was laughed at and ridiculed as being "paranoid." Flip the calendar forward fifty years and the picture is quite different. Now those same 1960s "liberals" and their intellectual heirs are constantly sounding the alarm bell that "the Russians are coming!" They sound like John Birchers in their obsessive fear and hatred of all things Russian. The Russians have not changed all that much, it's just that the vacillating nature of the American political culture is inconstant and largely devoid of any principled conviction. In this particular meta-game, Russians continue to play chess, while the Americans still play checkers. When we view the Chinese, we realize they are actually playing three-dimensional chess, with the addition of practical ideological or strategic elements drawn from the playbook of the Führer. The serious study of Bolshevistic Red Magic can help close that semiotic gap in our understanding.

# The Branches of the Root

In the Age of Putin, the Russian people have sustained more individual and group freedom than at any time in their history— at least since the days of the Rûs (Kingdom of Kiev). That a people without a long and recent tradition of individual liberty continue to have considerable problems adjusting to their new circumstances should not be surprising. The situation is volatile— and full of energy. Developments in Russia have to be counted as one of the most stimulating cultural stories being played out in the world today. Among the most exciting aspects is the fact that they have not violently put all dimensions of their past behind them, but rather seek to synthesize all aspects of that past into a new future. A re-synthesis of everything from their pagan heritage (in the lore of Rodnovery) to their Orthodox traditions and from Cosmism to Bolshevism holds out the promise of a powerful (and dangerous) alchemical product in the future.

Gary Lachman (2020: 6) points out that Vladimir Putin is a proponent of the philosophies of the Russian Silver Age. He gave a reading assignment to his governors consisting of works by Silver Age philosophers, e.g., Solovyov's *The Justification of the Good*, Beryaev's *The Philosophy of Inequality* and Ilyin's *Our Tasks*. Popular opinion in the West about Putin is quite myopic. Putin was a lieutenant colonel in the KGB stationed in Germany. He is a rather learned man and student of many things. He speaks several languages, is fluent in German and knows basic Tatar, Swedish and English. He can understand us, but few understand him. In many ways, Putin's aims are to use the Russian philosophies of the Silver Age and implement them in fresh ways in a new Russia. One thing is clear, Putin respects only strength and will take advantage of any perceived weakness.

## Alexandr Dugin

One individual who has been called Putin's "Rasputin" is Alexandr Gelyevich Dugin (born 1962). He is an esotericist, political analyst and strategist. His father was a colonel-general in the Soviet military intelligence, and although Dugin's own career did not follow traditional establishment patterns, he has served as an advisor to the Kremlin and has himself organized three different political parties: the National Bolshevik Party (NBP),(4) the National Bolshevik Front and the Eurasia Party. He is the author of more than thirty books. In the 1980s, Dugin was an anti-Communist dissident, helped organize the nationalist group Pamyat and after the fall of the USSR wrote the program for the new Communist Party of the Russian Federation. He openly admires what might be called the idealistic aspects of National Socialism.

Perhaps Dugin's most influential book is *Foundations of Geopolitics* (1997) which was used as a textbook at the Russian Academy of the General Staff. It promotes the Eurasian idea which is an exhortation of Russia to re-establish its empire, extending all the way to Dublin in the West and into Iran in the South. In that same year, he published a reassessment of fascism called "Fascism— Borderless and Red." In it he expresses admiration for aspects of National Socialism but envisions a new fascism without racism and chauvinistic nationalism. Dugin is also a great admirer of the Italian esotericist and Traditionalist Julius Evola.

As regards religion and the esoteric Dugin stands in the middle between Orthodoxy and Rodnovery, or Russian neo-paganism. In a formal sense, Dugin espouses adherence to the so-called Old Believers, an offshoot branch of the Russian Orthodox Church which rejects modern reforms of the 17th century. Organizations or religious ideologies with which he has shown great sympathy include Anastasianism and Ynglism. Such movements are linked with the idea of cultural integrity and an Indo-European context for spirituality which brings the Slavic, Iranian and Germanic cultures into their realm of understanding.

## Rodnovery

The Slavic world witnessed a great upsurge in a neo-pagan activity after the fall of Communism in the early 1990s. In many ways some of these countries, and especially Russia, were in a uniquely advantageous position to reawaken the pre-Christian spirit of their ancient forefathers. This is because folk-religion, called the Old Faith, or Old Believers, often carried on a continuous line of tradition leading back to pagan times. In various ways, the dual-faith period mentioned in section 2.2 never really went away. The Communist insistence on atheism did not wipe out the Russian Orthodox Church, but neither did it annihilate the old folk traditions that were deeply embedded in the culture of the countryside. The Bolsheviks had even originally been interested in using this tradition to their advantage. The importance of all of this is that when Communism fell away, the old ways were not only left to emerge once more, but they did so in a world that had been "prepared" for them by seventy years of official atheism and official hostility toward Christianity. The land had, in a sense, been purified for a new beginning. It is a fascinating story of how seventy years of official atheism was unable to wipe out neither God nor the gods and goddesses of the ancient pagan ways. This is the great cultural advantage of Russia and other eastern European countries which have such deep cultural roots. In the West, as devoted as it is to the newest and latest fad and gadgets, deep culture would not fare so well under a similar sustained attack. Several generations of official Communist control did not wipe away Russian culture, whereas in the West a few years of ideological control over the media and the educational system have seriously damaged the native cultures of several nations. In 2003, the Russian Ministry of Justice recognized over forty organized forms of Rodnovery, although this was probably only the tip of an iceberg.

Rodnovery is the most common designation in Russian for the continuation or revival of the indigenous Slavic (Russian) pagan tradition— the "old religion," if you will. The word literally means "indigenous faith." It is derived from the roots *rod-*, "indigenous, ancestral" as well as "genus, kin, or 'race'" and *vera*, "faith or religion."

Pan-Slavic mystics, philosophers and artists had built upon the pre-Christian heritage of Russia back in the 19th century and were a vital part of the cultural matrix at the dawn of both Cosmism and Bolshevism. When the USSR fell, the Slavic pagan heritage reemerged with new strength. Russia, and many of the lands which had become part of first the Russian Empire, and then the Soviet Union, were marked by a strong sense of continuity from the pre-Christian past— whether in Russia, the Ukraine, the Baltic states or Ossetia. A variety of movements arose in this spirit, and they are distinguished by a vibrant grass-roots expression. They cannot be reduced to any one set of doctrines or ideologies, and in this they mirror the spirit of the pagan past in which individual families, tribes, clans and bands were decisive— contrary to any sort of unified orthodoxy.

The almost seventy-five years of Soviet atheism and official hostility to the Orthodox Church and Christianity in general prepared the ground for a strong revival of paganism in that it caused widespread doubt and skepticism with regard to Christianity, but left the indigenous faith more or less in peace to be carried on privately in Russian households and within families. This circumstance has created a situation in many of the former Socialist states whereby the old religions have a level of acceptance and prestige unknown in the West— in Germany, Scandinavia, Britain, etc.

In an interesting, and perhaps unexpected, way the Russian and Norse traditions have found new common ground based on old affinities and origins. Christopher McIntosh in his book *Beyond the North Wind* (2019: 145-176) shows how the Norse element is being re-fused into the nativistic, pagan element in modern Russia today. This synthesis makes a good deal of sense, even if it at first glance seems incredible, given the apparent conflict between the German and Russian cultures in recent years. The new spiritual relationship is based on deeply shared roots and practical considerations. Of course, the Slavic and Germanic peoples share a common Indo-European root and both were secondarily greatly influenced by North Iranian peoples (Scythians, Sarmatians, etc.) in ancient times. The very name of Russia is based on that of the Scandinavian Rûs, Swedish Vikings, who traded and raided down the rivers of the lands that became Russia and founded the Kingdom of Kiev in 879. The practical dimension of the search for spiritual roots in the myths of the Norsemen is this: No other pagan people (including the Romans) have left a better record of their mythology and religious sentiments than the Norse. These aspects are mainly preserved in the Icelandic sagas and poetry. The modern revival of Norse religion, variously called Ásatrú, Odinism, "Heathenry," etc., has become a model for other such movements independent of the innovated or *ad hoc* efforts at "neo-paganism," "Wicca," etc. The Norse, some might call it Hyperborean, tradition is a ready-made fit for many modern Russians to embrace.

"Polarian" esotericism which speculates about the ancient civilizations which might have existed both at the northern and southern extremes of the Earth is somewhat supported by the geological fact that for ninety-percent of the Earth's history there were no ice-caps at either pole. We still live in what, in geological terms, can be called an "ice-age." Whatever cultures or civilizations existed in these climes in times immemorial have long since been scraped and ground away by the movements of the glacial ice caps.

Some in the West may be confused by the interest in present-day Russia in the Norse forms of paganism. I asked a Russian expert who writes under the name Askr Svarte about this and in a personal response he clarified the complex issue. First of all, the indigenous pagan tradition of Rodnovery is more popular than are the Norse-based forms, buy quite a bit. But Norse forms of paganism also enjoy considerable popularity. The factors that led to this have been identified as the wave of esoteric literature that began being published in Russia in the Post-Soviet era, the number of academic scholars in the latter years of the USSR who published on Norse topics, as well as esoteric runologists such as Anton Platov. In addition to this, there was some "right-wing" influence on the trend as well as the impact of historical reconstructionists. Beyond these influential patterns, there is also the close cultural connection between the Germanic and Slavic peoples, the role of the *varyags* (Rûs) in early Russian history (as well as the German connection with the Romanov Dynasty). The Slavic and Germanic peoples were neighbors for millennia. While we are aware of the recent historical conflicts between them, it must be understood that much of the time, as in most such relationships, connections tended to be mutually productive.

Askr Svarte also adds that the German figures such as Guido von List have "very low or zero authority" among present-day Russian esotericists.

In a personal comment the Russian expert in Norse tradition, Nedeszhda Rubinskaya, reported that it was the presence of the high-level mythology, which she saw lacking in the surviving East-Slavic material, that drew her to the Norse tradition as a practical and personal matter.

## Socialistic Sorcery in the West

While the Russian heirs to the Soviet Empire have made Bolshevism one element in a complex kaleidoscope aimed toward a more optimistic future, socialists in the West have incorporated Marxist structures for the sake of what seem on the face of it all to be extremely petty goals: the obtaining and maintaining of political and economic power for themselves personally and for their fellow club-members in a network of cliques shielded by the aura of a "moral high ground" of political correctness. The concept of political correctness itself, after having examined the Marxist roots of the concept, must also be observed as a tool for the practice of a sort of political sorcery.

For a long time, certain "socialists" in the West pointed to the Scandinavian countries as models for what they dreamed about enforcing in other countries from Britain to America. They have partially succeeded in both countries, but as always with very mixed results. America is far more socialist than many like to admit. But none of it is even slightly tinged with the Red aura of a "heroic" Revolution. Much of the Welfare State mentality of the Scandinavian countries has recently been called into question and in any event Sweden, Norway and Denmark have always been healthy, vibrant and prosperous free-market economies.

Marx created a theory, but it could not be implemented until men such as Lenin and Mao installed it through raw violence. So, the magic of the Marxist theory was never fully tested as a form of sorcery until it began being utilized in the cultural war in Western contexts: in academia, the media and in electoral politics.

What is often called "Cultural Marxism," a phrase used mostly by conservative critics, and the existence of which is generally strategically denied by orthodox Marxists, who insist on a purely materialistic, positivistic and economic basis for their theories, is nevertheless a real Marxist-based strategy— and their most successful one when pure violence and coercion are removed from the equation. Cultural Marxism is expressed actively thought two schools of thought, the Frankfurt School and the adherents to and practitioners of, the hegemonic theory of Antonio Gramsci (1891-1937) the early 20th century Italian Communist leader.

Gramsci first analyzed hegemony as a description of how the capitalist establishment (the bourgeoisie) maintains its hold on power— by controlling in a hegemonic fashion the means of education, communication and civil bureaucracy, for example. This control meant that there was an entrenched cultural norm projected through these instruments into the culture generally. The values of the bourgeoisie became accepted and appeared "self-evident" to the population. This identity of the masses with these values prevented any overt rebellion, and hence thwarted any Revolution. The establishment controlled the newspapers (and what we would call "media" today), the school-system and the governmental bureaucracies.

From this analysis, Gramsci theorized that the answer for Revolutionaries in the West lies in the development of answers to these cultural institutions and the slow take-over, not of the *government* as such, but of the *culture* first, then the government will follow in a Western "democracy" as a matter of course. Interestingly, Gramsci also theorized that Marxism was a synthesis of Italian Renaissance humanism and the German Reformation and that Marxism could only overcome the status quo if it developed a new "religion:" that met the people's psychological needs.

The so-called Frankfurt School of Critical Theory was founded in 1929 at the University of Frankfurt in Germany. It was designed to promote socialist ideology and revolution by means of strategies alternative to the violent methods of Leninism. One of the chef proponents of the school, Max Horkheimer, explained that "critical theory" is comprised of three *criteria*: it must be simultaneously "explanatory, practical, and normative." That is, it must explain things in some revelatory manner (whereupon the hearer is awakened [= "woke"] to the "truth"), it must have methods of implementing itself in real life, and it must succeed in convincing the society that it is establishing a "new normal."

Even those on the Left sometimes poke fun at the Frankfurt School, calling it the "Frankfurt School of Witchcraft and Wizardry." This is largely because they spend their efforts making theoretical statements of extreme obscurity and questionable reality. Be that as it may, their obscure mutterings and theoretical word spinning have the practical and magical effect of helping those who use their formulas get and retain power in various political bodies, e.g. university departments. One does not need to repeat the story of how nonsense papers can be presented to the elite of academia, who do not understand the work (because it is has been intentionally composed to be unintelligible) but who nevertheless give it the highest praise, simply because they do not want to be thought of as being stupid by their colleagues.

To return to the idea of "political correctness" and sorcery: Let it be said that there is a kind of "Red Magic of Political Correctness." This sort of magic hinges on the use of individuals or groups which fall into a "protected class"— an oppressed minority, ethnic group, gender, etc., who, when they can be utilized as means of obtaining a "moral high ground" in a political or more usually economic struggle, the practitioner of Red Magic can gain material advantage through the technique. It is rather a corollary of Sun Tzu's admonition to fight only from the high ground on the field of battle. The high ground here is a "moral" one— and this morality is usually dependent upon the target's anxiety about being "fair" or "just." (The more the potential victim of Red Magic is saddled with a conscience or desire to "do the good" the more effective the sorcery will be.) It should be noted that this kind of sorcery is usually practiced most effectively, and ironically, by individuals who do not themselves fall into the category of any oppressed group. The most likely successful practitioners of Red Magic are well-educated, upper class white males who represent themselves as the "champions" of the cause of the oppressed victims of society. They "farm" the oppressed for profit, power and self-satisfied glory. Almost without exception these practitioners of the Red Magic of Political Correctness are not heroic men of the people, but rather those who have just hit upon a trick that works in today's world for obtaining and maintaining power (political power which is translated into individual and personal economic gain and prosperity). The aura of the Red Magic of Political Correctness wraps its practitioners in an impenetrable armor and provides them with the sheen of an appearance of superior morality and intelligence. It has always been a part of the Bolshevik technique to insist that their theories are the *only* intelligent and scientifically based ones and that all others are ignorant and just plain *incorrect*. (This particular sorcery goes all the way back to Marx and his original idea that he had *discovered* some law of the universe in the historical dialectic or historical materialism. In fact, the Marxist is not more intelligent than his opponent, except insofar as he is smart enough to insist that he is the only intelligent one in the room before anyone else has even had a chance to speak! As Nietzsche had already warned us, there is no longer truth and falsehood, only those who can argue better than others. And Nietzsche could have also told us what the nature of the game of the Bolshevik is: *Power*.

This brings us to another dimension of the practice of Red Magic: The necessity of up-and-coming aspirants to power within the Revolutionary framework to be able to curry the favor of those of higher rank within the movement. Once a Bolshevik system is even partially in place, there occurs a process of convincing those with some power in the system to promote lower echelon members to higher positions within that system. This usually involves demonstrations of knowledge of the ideology or the Party, loyalty to it and to the higher-ranking members, or at least signaling that one is in agreement with the general ideology of the group. This is necessary to be what the mob would call becoming a "made man." In a Stalinist world, a person's very life could depend on this.

There have actually been a number of strategies for the assumption of the reins of power in the American body politic. Among these is the so-called Cloward-Piven Strategy. Cloward and Piven were professors of sociology at Columbia University in the 1960s. They actually wrote about their strategy in an article published in *The Nation* magazine in 1966. The article was entitled "The Weight of the Poor: A Strategy to End Poverty." This was not so much a "strategy to end poverty" as it was a tactic to collapse the capitalist system by sowing economic and cultural *chaos* and over-loading the capacity of any system in the society to care for its ever-increasing client-citizenry. The key to this form of sorcery is to overload or swamp any system one wishes to control and to be prepared to take advantage of the chaos caused by this maneuver. Once the system collapses, a socialist program can be more easily instituted. Of course, this strategy is keyed to the host culture's establishment having any compassion for the plight of the "poor." It would not consequently work in a state such as found at present in North Korea.

The magical or sorcerous use of language is all around us today. Both the Russian Bolsheviks and the German National Socialists were fairly skilled in these arts. On the American political scene, generally Democrats are somewhat skilled at this, Republicans and "conservatives" generally are for the most part hopeless dullards and simpletons, although Trump could wield words like an Abrams Tank. Crude, but effective, examples of Democrats using this technique is effected by calling one of their candidates "the world's smartest woman," or another "the most eloquent speaker" when in fact there was really never any objective or factual evidence that either of these things was true about either person. But the seed was planted and the *perception* was established through the use and repetition of magical word-formulas alone. These are concrete and easy to understand examples of this principle of sorcery in action.

## Magical Marxism

Especially young people in the West have been continually prepared by their educational system, *à la* Gramsci, to accept, and even embrace, the labels of Marxism and Socialism. However, it probably does not need to be pointed out that the conditions under which these largely affluent and profoundly "schooled" individuals live hardly bears much resemblance to the lives of early 20th century Russians, Germans or any other working class Europeans (or even Americans). Therefore, it is inevitable that Marxism itself would have to be transformed by the host into which it is being received. In this process, it can be seen that the ideas of the Cosmists bear far more similarity to the temperament of the new contemporary Western generation than they do to the rough and tumble gang-land world of the Russian Bolsheviks. Clearly current would-be Marxists are sometimes being guided by "old school" Bolsheviks in their tactics, but the long-term prognosis for such tactics seems limited in cultures from France, to Germany to the USA steeped as they are in the atmosphere of individual liberty and economic comfort.

At the same time, ideas and practices that border on the magical have become mainstream in the thought processes of the contemporary younger generation. Meditation, new-thought, new-age, self-help and the notion that humans can alter their reality by altering their thoughts and through what have come to be called "memes" have all become parts of consensus reality for a majority of people in the West. This combination of factors has led to the inception of something that might be called "magical Marxism." There is even a book by that title by Andy Merrifield.

# 6. General Conclusion and Assessment

Throughout this book, we have seen examples of how ideology can come to destroy, or greatly disrupt, the results and findings of science, for example. This is not limited to the humanities, where the effects of ideology can have immediate and profound effects due to the fact that "truth" is usually constructed out of a consensus of the opinions of "experts," but in the hard sciences as well, e.g. matters affecting climate change or virology. General failure and collapse will always follow if rational and scientific thought is subjected to political or ideological criteria. This led to the collapse of the hegemony of Christianity at the dawn of the modern age, and certainly brought the Soviet Union down. This is a warning that seems rarely headed today.

The roots of Bolshevism were planted in some of the most radical intellectual matrices in the history of man. These roots had certain effects on the shape of Bolshevism, but a definite and determinative ideological orthodoxy surrounding historical materialism continually reared its head to destroy any real progress these bold new ideas dared to attempt to actualize. Just as there is a class of intellectual morons in the world — those people who allow their thinking to be dominated unquestioningly by certain fashionable and socially acceptable *templates* — so too can whole political structures suffer from ideological moronity. The Nazis fell victim to it, as did the Bolsheviks.

The word "socialism" has undergone a number of mutations over the years. At the dawn of the $21^{st}$ century the old heroic socialism expressed by the Bolsheviks, for example, is rarely found. The Chinese learned some new tricks from the Bolsheviks, but they remain, well, Chinese in all regards. The old Emperor just has a new religion. Small states such as North Korea, Cuba or Vietnam are only interested in the survival of their regimes or the personal survival and continued empowerment of their leaders. In Europe, many countries formerly under Socialist rule in the East Bloc have become paragons of freedom and republicanism. Former welfare states in Scandinavia have abandoned as much as possible their socialist baggage. Only in the USA does it seem that the *idea* of "socialism" is fashionably on the rise in certain circles. But the heroic Bolsheviks of then or now do not recognize this form of thought as having much to do with theirs. Heroic Bolshevism is motivated to transform the world, to transform the human race and to do things formerly thought only possible for *God* or the *gods*. It aims to make mankind into a race of immortal and omnipotent

117

god-like entities. The socialism being sold in the USA today is a "socialism" for *victims*, real or imagined, always under the sponsorship and guidance of a political "master class." These new masters, these new "nobles," are now ensconced in political bureaucracies, academia and in the corporate boardrooms of multi-national companies. The "victims" who are their clients and for whom they claim to "work," are an interesting lot. These are victims of nature, society or history who have been enchanted into becoming the clients of this bureaucratic class of apparatchiks all of whom farm their client-base as a fiefdom of political and economic power in the open fields of representative democracy. Rendering the clients dependent upon the apparatchiks, or more precisely convincing the clients that they are utterly dependent upon the activity of these apparatchiks for their survival or "happiness" is the key. The availability of the fruits of the labor of productive members of society remains a gold mine of limited resources— the goose that lays the golden egg. Only if the victim client-base, combined in a coalition with the apparatchiks themselves, exceeds 50% on a permanent basis is economic stability assured. This form of socialism again has little to do with that of the Old Bolsheviks who heroically took power by force and tried to install a heroic futuristic vision. The common socialism of today mainly appears to be a mode for the better educated and already reasonably affluent to make use of the less-well-educated and economically marginal as a vote-farm in a Devil's bargain by which the well-educated receive and maintain cushy jobs and the clients receive a steady stream of "crumbs." It is questionable whether the *heroic* form of Bolshevism will ever be seen again, the new client-based form pays too well, with minimum risk.

The original Bolsheviks used the idea and reality of the "proletariat" (workers or working class) as their client-base. In places such as Russia workers and peasants (former serfs) constituted what appeared to have become a permanently oppressed sub-class. In the advanced democratic republics of the industrialized West, this class simply did not exist, or if they did they did not identify as an oppressed sub-class in need of sponsorship by a Party elite to survive or thrive. The Bolsheviks (and even for a time the Empire of Japan) attempted to target racial minorities in the USA as a substitute for the Proletariat. This too did not work at first. But eventually, applying the principles expounded by Gramsci, the image of a permanently oppressed sub-class with no hope of survival without the sponsorship of, and intervention by, an elite cadre of apparatchiks ensconced in a governmental bureaucracy began to get traction. Then and there, as here and now, the apparatchiks only rarely ever belong the

118

"oppressed" sub-class themselves. The essence of Red Magic is the replacement of one aristocracy with another— although this reality must be kept as one of its greatest secrets.

But in the end who knows what *history* will bring us. The milk-toast approaches of Western "democratic socialism" may just be preparing us on the way toward the reemergence of a new and powerful, and most importantly, *heroic*, form of socialism in which the theories of Cosmism and Marxism will finally be wedded together to usher in a new phase of human existence that will ultimately transcend the limitations of this planet. In any event, we cannot expect that the orthodox Marxist philosophy of economics or history will prove any more valid in the future than it has in the past. But the deeper roots out of which Bolshevism originally grew may yet bear fruit in the Russian Motherland.

# Appendix
## Esoteric Bolshevism and Zoroastrian Tradition

At first it is again shocking to think that the most ancient universal religion, that was first promulgated by the Prophet Zarathustra as early as 1700 BCE, and the scientific theories of Russian Cosmists and even those political and economic ideas of early Bolshevists in Russia could have anything in common. But a close examination reveals a different story.

It should be recalled at this point that the Iranian world and that of eastern, central and northern Europe actually vigorously intersected throughout the last two millennia BCE, well into the first millennium CE, from about 700 BCE to 500 CE. Sometimes they battled against one another, but more often than not they worked and fought cooperatively alongside each other. The art-forms of Europeans, the Celts and Germanic peoples especially, were greatly influenced by the northern Iranian (e.g. Scythian and Sarmatian) styles. This indicates a deep-level fertilization by Iranian culture. Many mythic concepts and images from these Iranian peoples shaped Germanic mythology, e.g. cosmology and eschatology. The contrasting deities representing white and black, good and evil, are pronounced in Slavic mythology and are thought by many to have been an influence from Iranian sources, in emphasis, at least.

As we will see here, however, the influence — or is it *resonance* — between ancient Iranian and Russian Cosmist thinking perhaps goes much deeper into the levels of profound philosophical thinking.

As we have seen throughout this book, the Russian Cosmists proposed the perfection and immortalization of all individuals of the past and present and, as is well-known, the transformation of the Earth (and other planets) into heavenly realms in which not only every individual would be happy, but also every atom of everything would actually achieve *happiness*! How was this to be done? By miracles of God? No! By the application of human reason and enlightenment through technology. The Cosmists were well-aware that this achievement had miraculous components, but that it was after all the great plan of the universe, guided by consciousness that man and man alone was the agent by which this achievement, this "common task," could actually be completed.

Zarathustra was the first to teach that everything was evolving according to a plan. It was from his teachings that the early Jews acquired this idea, which they might have called "God's Plan."

The text below is one that I wrote in 2014, long before I had much of any idea about Russian Cosmism. The similarities between this most ancient of mythologies and Cosmism are striking. But this presentation, I think, only scratches the surface of what is there:

Just as the individual meets an end, so too will the whole cosmic order. The doctrine of Zarathustra introduced the idea of a final end to time, a final end to history, and end resulting in an ultimate perfection.

In order to perfect the world Ahura Mazda created Time (Zurvan) so that certain Ages of Time could be segmented and thus events could more easily be controlled and guided. An end-time was set by Ahura Mazda in order to limit the power of destruction and chaos, just as you might set certain goals and deadlines in life, or even in your day in order that things are accomplished in a timely manner. The goal is for consciousness to rule time, not for time to overwhelm consciousness. Eventually the world will mature into a perfected state through a combination of the innate patterns established by the Creator, Ahura Mazda, the functions of the Amesha Spentas, the *yazatas* and the efforts of the *fravashis* of humanity consciously working toward the perfection and permanence of the good world order.

An important and influential myth emerging from the Mazdan and Zarathushtran tradition is that of the advent of world-saviors. This myth holds that various human heroes have been born and will be born into this world who have helped and who will help guide mankind toward the final perfection of the world, the Frashokereti, or "Making-Wonderful." These are called Saoshyants there have been several of these in history, chief among them Zarathustra himself. In the final time of this cycle the ultimate Saoshyant will perform certain rites and accomplish certain things to complete the perfection of the world. Of course, the relationship of humanity to these *saoshyants* is not passive, mankind is not supposed to merely await action to occur from above, the works and workings of individual human beings are actually necessary to invoke the change-making force. In other words, magic is necessary.

In the fulfillment of time everything that has ever been created by Lord Wisdom will be remanifested in an immortal and perfect form, individuals and true nations will be reconstituted in their ideal forms. This is a testimony to the high regard the Mazdan tradition has for the world of matter and of the flesh. Not only will humans be immortal in spirit, but in body also. The logic of this is that whatever Lord Wisdom created in the spirit and matter was originally perfect, and it is this state of perfection, spiritual and material, that it is logically destined to manifest.

*Original Magic* pp. 34-35

It becomes clear that the final state of existence as seen from an orthodox Zoroastrian and from a Cosmist and even Marxist perspective are virtually identical. In this it is perhaps also most noteworthy that humanity is the chief active agent in this process. As opposed to the version of this myth employed by Judeo-Christian religion which sees man as an impotent bystander in it all, and God and only God as the active agent in the outcome, the ancient Iranian and Cosmist view is that man is here, either as a placement by the Wise Lord or as a product of evolution, as the active and potent element in the cosmos. Humanity will use magic (Zoroastrian religion) and science (rational employment of the mind to solve problems) to effect (or aid in the effecting) of the Frashokereti— in which all is made "wonderful," or some say "juicy."

One well-known scholar of Zoroastrianism, R. C. Zaehner, summed up the its philosophy as being one of "creative evolution" dedicated to the idea of the "continuous evolution toward the Making Excellent." Significantly, this evolution is not something which just occurs naturally, but rather it is something that humans have to work at and fight for. Humans are an indispensable, necessary and active agent in this process.

Curiously, there was a Zoroastrian "heresy" which flourished in the 3rd to 6th centuries in pre-Islamic Iran, and to which certain emperors paid some attention and Kavâd I, whom we met when discussing Stalin's knick-name, likely converted to the sect and promoted it within the Arabic kingdom of Al-Hirah in Mesopotamia. It was called the Mazdakite sect. Its founder was Mazdak. Mazdak was an ancient Revolutionary, with subsequent figures also taking his name. Mazdak taught both altruism and hedonism. All pleasures were indulged and appetites satisfied, in what he called a "spirit of equality." He further taught that followers should avoid the shedding of blood and harming other beings. Vegetarianism was practiced. They were also supposed to practice a high level of hospitality. Although Mazdakites were charged with "sharing women," many scholars today doubt this. But they do seem to have had a doctrine of "free love." They are considered to have been the first true socialists placing all property in common and benefitting all. Mazdakite cosmology viewed the mixture of Light and Dark, Sprit and Matter in a more optimistic way than the Manicheans.

The Mazdakites reduced the formalities of religious ritual, placing more emphasis on ethics and correct living. In this they revolted against the established professional Zoroastrian priesthood.

In the Mazdakite version of economic history originally there was enough wealth and goods to be shared equally. But the stronger soon learned to coerce the weaker and a great disparity and inequality resulted. Theologically this was explained that the five *divs* (demons") of Envy, Anger, Vengeance, Need and Greed were greatly empowered— so Mazdak's system of ethics was instituted to defeat these trends. It was Mazdak's plan to have all excess wealth redistributed. He wanted to put an end to the "next of kin marriages" practiced by wealthy Zoroastrians in order to keep property in their family-lines. Women too were to be redistributed, and not hoarded by wealthy princes in polygamous arrangements.

As we know Marx wrote his doctoral dissertation in philosophy on the Greek Epicureans, who posited the atomic theory of pure materialism. It has been widely thought that teachers (*magûs*) from Persia or elsewhere in the Persian Empire first taught the Greeks about this theory. The Greeks, like other Western thinkers after them, dichotomized the ideas so that materialism excluded the "spiritual." This same pattern would be found in the 18th century forward among those in the West who developed sympathies for the Devil. The mistaken and myopic model of spirit *versus* matter, which had really been created by Christian theology with its strict dichotomy between God (the Creator) and nature (the Created). This strict dichotomy too may indeed have its roots in Iranian thinking as well in the form of Manicheanism— a religion to which St. Augustine, the main father of Christian philosophy or theology belonged in his youth. There Matter is *evil* and the Spirit *good*. Although this system had its roots in Iranian thought, it is the most repugnant of heresies among the *orthodox* Zoroastrians because it impugns the glorious material creation of Lord-Wisdom and his Co-Workers (*hamkars*) with evil. In fact, as we have seen pure matter as originally created by Lord-Wisdom, is just as "good" as is the spiritual realm also stemming from the same source of consciousness.

The morality of Bolshevism and that of orthodox Zoroastrianism are very similar: that which is good is that which promotes or furthers progress toward a perfected state of being — for the Bolsheviks Communism and for the Zoroastrians *Frashokereti*. To the Bolshevik such good actions are called Revolutionary, actions which divert progress away from perfection are called Counter-Revolutionary or "reactionary."

The enormous difference between Zoroastrianism and Bolshevism is that the philosophy of Zarathustra holds that there is a spiritual realm, and that it precedes the physical and material manifestation of the world. However, the good part of this creation is considered in no way "inferior" to the spiritual aspect. Both are *equally* holy. There are many more differences that that, of course. But here we are just taking a look at what is similar between them.

The Old Bolsheviks, the Heroic Bolsheviks, perhaps had a chance at arriving at a way of thinking which would have entered the Cosmist mindscape akin to the ideology of Zarathustra, transcending the original limits of Marxism. However, history, contrary to Marxist theory did not lead to a more perfect understanding, but rather collapsed into itself according to a Stalinist authoritarian model. This occurred as "historical materialism" was codified in such a way that ignored the Cosmist philosophical dimension and fell back on primitive notions of crude materialism and violent coercion with no hope of real evolutionary change. As this process reached its sterile conclusion, the cause was eventually lost. But now, after this failure, perhaps a braver new generation can take up the old Cosmist dreams and a new understanding can be the foundation for a new beginning. Even the Soviets eventually began to realize what they had lost. As early as the 1960s there were efforts underway to revive the Cosmist cause. But it was too little too late.

There is a clear dichotomy between good and evil in most philosophical systems, even those that try to deny the existence of such a dichotomy. The thought of Friedrich Nietzsche clearly is not "beyond" considerations of good and evil, i.e. good and bad on one level — as he clearly rails against so much in the world that is *bad*, and extols the virtues of other things that are *good*. His objection is really more against the *conventional*, orthodox and dogmatic designations. In philosophical, and hence Mazdan terms, we can identify those things that are good are characterized by the qualities of strength, vitality, continuity and effectiveness. Those things that are bad damage these qualities. The dichotomy is so often misunderstood by ancient dualistic sects (such as the Manicheans) as well as by most modern followers of Marx as that of an antipathy between "spirit" and "matter." This was never part of the Mazdan model, as matter and spirit, although they exist equally, are equally either good or evil. The key is that they both emerge from the one source: *energy*. This energy, in order to be dynamic, requires polarity within its core, hence exists Ahura-Mazda: "lord-wisdom." Russian Marxism-Leninism had the potential to emerge from its initial form and evolve in a Revolutionary manner based on its roots in Cosmism. The elements were there, but they were crushed under the thuggery of Stalin. It must be noted, however, that history shows that the *tragedy* was that Russia needed Stalin in order to survive Operation Barbarossa. The better future in which, through the tempests the sun of freedom, could have shone to them would have been free of both Uncle Joe and the threat of Hitler so that a more Cosmist future could perhaps have unfolded.

# Notes

(1) Russian Cosmism is not to be confused with the philosophy of the American writer of weird fiction, H. P. Lovecraft, who referred to his own approach as "Cosmicist." Cosmicism is an atheistic philosophy which holds that the cosmos is entirely indifferent even to the very existence of humanity.

(2) A realistic and thoroughgoing exploration of the occult in connection with the Nazis is offered in my as-yet unpublished manuscript entitled *The Occult in National Socialism*. Nicholas Goodrick-Clarke's book *The Occult Roots of Nazism* (Aquarian, 1985) is a reputable work, but one that it too limited in its scope to explain the topic is purports to cover. Goodrick-Clarke focused almost entirely on the nationalist, or *völkisch* elements of Nazism, and that of the apparently "neo-pagan" sort as well. Other occult aspects, e.g. occult sciences, technologies, etc. are ignored.

(3) For a review of this process in the Germanic world, see my projected three-volume study *The Northern Dawn*, of which the first volume has appeared with Arcana Europa (2017).

(4) The term "National Bolshevism" was first coined as *Nationalbolschewismus* by German followers of Ernst Niekisch around 1926. It represented a form of Socialism in line with nationalistic, rather than economic or class-based categories. Another notable supporter was Ernst Jünger. The roots of National Bolshevism were in the Communist Workers' Party of Germany. In the 1920s Nikolai Ustialov adopted the German term for use among Russian who were revolutionary, but not "communist" in the usual sense, having their principal loyalty to Russia and the cause of Pan-Slavicism. For a brief while the concept was revived in current Russian political life by Alexandr Dugin.

# Bibliography

Bakunin, Mikail. *God and the State*. New York: Dover, 1970.

Berlin, Isiah. *Karl Marx*. Oxford: Oxford University Press, 1963.

Bogdanov, Alexander. *Red Star: The First Bolshevik Utopia*. Trans. Charles Rougle, ed. L. R. Graham and R. Stites. Bloomington: Indiana University Press, 1984.

Daim, Wilfried. *Der Mann, der Hitler die Ideen gab*. Munich: Isar.1958

Flowers, Stephen E. *Original Magic*. Rochester: Inner Traditions, 2017.

——————————. *The Occult in National Socialism*. Rochester: Inner Traditions, 2022.

Fulop-Miller, René. *The Mind and Face of Bolshevism: An Examination of Cultural Life in Soviet Russia*. Trans. F. S. Flint & D. F. Tait. London: G. P. Putnam's Sons, 1927.

Glatzer Rosenthal, Bernice, ed. *The Occult in Russian and Soviet Culture*. Ithaca: Cornell University Press, 1997.

Groberg, Kristi A. "The Shade of Lucifer's Dark Wing: Satanism in Silver Age Russia." In: Bernice Glatzer Rosenthal, ed. *The Occult in Russian and Soviet Culture*. Ithaca: Cornell University Press, 1997, pp. 99-133.

Groys, Boris, ed. *Russian Cosmism*. Cambridge: MIT Press, 2018.

Gutkin, Irina. "The Magic of Words." In: Bernice Glatzer Rosenthal, ed. *The Occult in Russian and Soviet Culture*. Ithaca: Cornell University Press, 1997, pp. 225-246.

Hagemeister, Michael. "Russian Cosmism in the 1920s and Today." In: *The Occult in Russian and Soviet Culture*. Ithaca: Cornell University Press, 1997, pp. 185-202.

Kolakowski, Leszek. *Main Currents of Marxism: I: The Founders*. Oxford: Oxford University Press, 1981.

Kravchinsky, Sergei M. *The Russian Peasantry: Their Agrarian Condition, Social Life, and Religion*. Westport, CT: Hyperion, 1977 [1888].

Lachman, Gary. *The Return of Holy Russia*. Rochester: Inner Traditions, 2020.

Lagalisse, Erica. *Occult Features of Anarchism*. Oakland: PM Press, 2019.

McIntosh, Christopher. *Beyond the North Wind*. Newburyport: Weiser, 2019.

Magee, Glenn Alexander. *Hegel and the Hermetic Tradition*. Ithaca: Cornell University Press, 2001.

LaVey, Anton Szandor. *The Satanic Rituals*. New York: Avon, 1972.

Menzel, Birgit, et al., eds. *The New Age of Russia: Occult and Esoteric* Dimensions. Munich: Lang, 2012.

Merrifield, Andy. *Magical Marxism: Subversive Politics and the Imagination.* London: Pluto Press, 2011.

Nowak, Pawel and Rafal Zimny. "Joseph Stalin's statements on language and linguistics as verbal acts of autocracy." *Oblicza Kommunikacji* 7 (2014), pp. 67-74.

Ostrander, Sheila ad Lynn Schroeder. *Psychic Discoveries Behind the Iron Curtain.* New York: Bantam, 1971.

Pospielovsky, Dimitry V. *A History of Marxist-Leninist Atheism and Soviet Anti-Religious Policies, A History of Soviet Atheism in Theory, and Practice, and the Believer*, Vol 1. New York: St. Martin's Press, 1987.

Pearlman, Ellen. "The Resurgence of Russian Cosmism." *PAJ: A Journal of Performance and Art.* 122 (2019), pp. 85-92.

Riemer, Neal. *Karl Marx and Prophetic Politics.* New York: Praeger, 1987.

Rosenthal, Bernice Glatzer, ed. *The Occult in Russian and Soviet Culture.* Ithaca: Cornell University Press, 1997.

Rummpel, R. J. *Lethal Politics: Soviet Genocide and Mass Murder since 1917.* London: Routledge, 2017.

Tsiolkovsky, Konstantin. "Panpsychicism, or Everything Feels." In: Boris Groys, ed. *Russian Cosmism* [1925]. Cambridge: MIT Press, 2018, pp. 113-155.

Webb, James. *The Harmonious Circle.* New York: Putnam, 1980.

Young, George M. *The Russian Cosmists: The Esoteric Futurism of Nikolai Fedorov and his Followers.* Oxford: Oxford University Press, 2012.

Znamenski, Andrei. *Red Shambhala.* Wheaton: Quest, 2011.

To find more interesting books by the author go to:
## www.seekthemysteries.com

www.ingramcontent.com/pod-product-compliance
Lightning Source LLC
Chambersburg PA
CBHW010041090426
42734CB00019B/3244